This book is dedicated to
the conscious awareness in the
heart of all humanity.

Invisible

Invisible

A Society of Prisons

An Opportunity for Dialogue

Valerie M. Malla

Poppy Publishing, Ltd.
www.poppypublishing.ca

Poppy Publishing, Ltd.

For additional information (such as educational discounts on bulk printings) please contact:
Poppy Publishing, P.O. Box 2334, 495 W. Georgia Street, Vancouver, BC V6B 3W2, Canada

Visit: www.poppypublishing.ca

Authored & Designed by: Valerie M. Malla
Moral rights of the author are asserted.

First Printing, Paperback, 2024
Printed in Canada.

Maintained @ Library of Archives Canada
ISBN 13: 978 1990 244 001 (pbk)
ISBN 13: 978 1990 244 018 (ebk)

10 9 8 7 6 5 4 3 2 1

Poppy Publishing, Ltd.
www.poppypublishing.ca

Acknowledgements

I appreciate everyone who supported the making of this book,
and all the resources that made it possible.

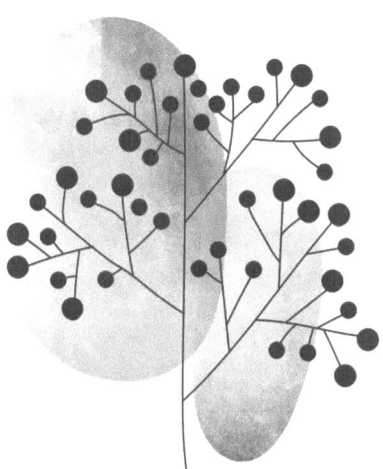

Author's Preface

The reason for the publication of this book is to provide a starting point for dialogue regarding several issues in how we are socialized as human beings, and specifically in how they relate to the incarceration of human beings, and the question of incarceration itself; and even to the extent of how we are all incarcerated in different ways due to our social systems.

The strong argument that has dominated for centuries in the western world is that we have built, and utilize prisons in which to hold offenders, because we do not have an alternate system. There also is the issue of complexities in the legal system, blame and punishment for perceived wrongs and crimes, and of course, morality.

What are the appropriate responses to disruptive, threatening, or violent behaviour? And have we truly considered all the variables to those questions and answers? As a society, we entrust and rely on learned individuals to think critically, and implement the best remedies, simply because the issues are so complex that the average person is arguably not available to respond in a comprehensive manner. Ironically, it is on the *support* of the average person — the "public" — that the learned rely when laws and decisions are made. But, is it a fair and appropriate attribution to rest on the support of a public that is not informed or prepared to adequately respond to such complex questions? In this way, is the support real, valid, and sound?

It is the intention of this book to provide basic context from which individuals and communities may begin to contemplate on these matters that affect everyone. Indeed, all of society is effected by the foundations that are laid in law, whether social or political. These effects are worth our consideration.

The sections presented in this book (Sections 1 - 4) include various angles from which to locate, ponder, question, and contemplate the issues. Take your time to review not only the many variables to consider (biology, blame, religion, politics, lables and categories, family, economic, social circumstances, and rehabilitation, etc.), but also the manner in which they all inter-relate, and the real consequential impact on individuals and society as a whole. It is well beyond the scope of this book to provide a comprehensive look at all the potential variables under scrutiny, but it is a starting point — a point of reference from which dialogues and discussions may take place, and further equiry may be inspired.

Applying broad-spectrum critical thinking skills to the various areas presented in this book and beyond, is the privilege of the reader. And it is no understatement that, as a human, one of the greatest satisfactions in life is to fully grasp meaning and purpose, so that it may aid in navigating the world for the best possible outcomes.

Due to the fact that we construct our personal reality through our perceptions, values, beliefs, norms, justifications, laws, and traditions, so also do we construct our greater world. And, underlying these are our emotions and rationale working in tandem. By questioning how we have come to hold the views we have and make the choices we make, this book presents the opportunity to evaluate our inner awareness as it relates to our outer experiences: intra-personally and inter-personally.

It is no small aim that I, as philosopher and author, have very deliberately put forth that philosophical enquiry is the most important tool we have as humans to gain insight into the deepest aspects of our existence, and thereby, affect change.

Make sure to have fun and enjoy the process! Whether you are reading this text as a personal endeavour, or participating in a group dialogue, the process is almost the same. Dialogue is not debate. Dialogue creates a space to contemplate and consider varying perspectives, which will take time — and that is its gift. Dialogue is not rushed. Rather, it allows one time to think, without judgement or pressure, and aids in not reaching a quick and hasty conclusion.

One example of the manner in which to approach the prompts for dialogue in this book, is the manner you would intuitively use to examine the following perplexing condition:

How and why is it the case that many humans live one reality of life wanting retribution for transgressions great or small; yet, another seeking entertainments depicting indecencies and violent or vulgar expressions?

Indeed, if dialogue were practiced more often, we may have very different norms, traditions, systems, expectations (and personal experiences) than we do today. I wish you all the best in your exploration!

Most sincerely,
~Valerie M. Malla

"We are all implicated when we allow other people to be mistreated. An absence of compassion can corrupt the decency of a community, a state, a nation."

~ *Bryan Stevenson*
Author, "Just Mercy"

"Just remember that your real job is that if you are free, you need to free somebody else.
If you have some power, then your job is to empower somebody else."

~ Toni Morrison (1931-2019)
Author & Humanist

Table of Contents: *Reader's Guide*

Section 1
History & Definitions

 I-I9

The first section provides an overview into the origins of prisons and their systems in the UK, Canada, and USA.

Although the history is deliberately not comprehensive, its purpose is to provide for you some general context in which to apply the sections that follow.

Explore and research beyond this book (*begin with the resources cited throughout this book, and in the References & Resources section starting on p. 120*).

Section 2
Philosophical Insights

 27-39

One of the greatest challenges to any human system is its design. This section puts forth some philosophical thoughts on underlying human issues.

Notice whether you agree or disagree and why. Then, try developing your own reasons and philosophy!

Section 3

Real Life Stories

47-83

In this section, the reader will encounter real-life stories of persons incarcerated.

Some of the stories are nearly forgotten in history, whilst others are more recent as of this book's publication.

A special focus on *youth incarceration* is included.

Section 4

Possibilities

91-111

Some suggestions have been offered in this section for future directions.

You may come up with many more possibilities yourself throughout the ongoing process of contemplation, and dialogue with others.

Use your creative imagination on how you can interest others with dialogue on this topic!

But from the Holy Land soon came
    Returning pilgrims there,
And heavy tidings brought with them
    For Margaret's anxious ear.

For Wenzel is a captive made
    In Paynim dungeon cold,
And there must lie till ransom paid
    A hundred coins of gold.

Alas for Margaret ! should she spin,
    And all her store be sold,
In one long year she scarce could win
    A single piece of gold.

Yet love can hope through good and ill,
    When other hope is gone ;
Shall she who loves so well be still,
    And he in prison groan ?

125

A Prisoner, by William Dyce, London 1846
British Library Archives

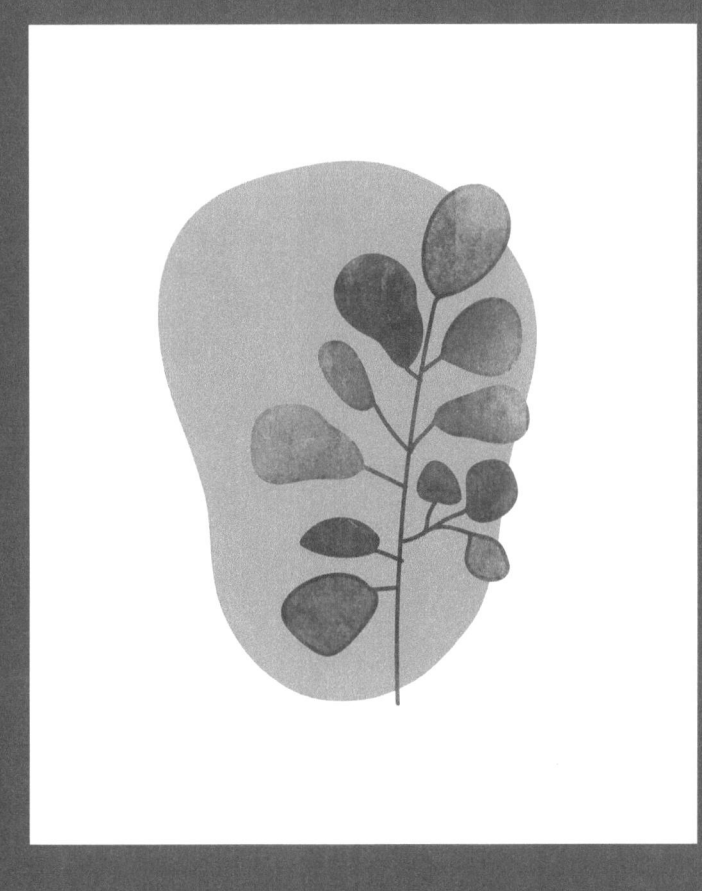

"Transformation in the criminal justice system can't
just take place with the offenders. It's also got to be
those of us working in the system,
and society at large."

~ *Robert Barton, California Inspector General*
"transformation of the broken criminal justice system",
TEDxSanQuentin, 2017

I

History & Definitions
Groundwork

The origin of prisons is a massive topic. In spite this and respecting this, the information contained in this book focuses primarily on similarities of penal systems in some countries of what is termed the 'western world': America, Britain, and Canada; and only to the extent that it provide a summary foundation in order to begin the process of contemplation and dialogue. To investigate beyond the initial information contained in this book, one will need to go through the research channels available to them, such as online resources or an in-person library. There are also many resources made available at the end of this book to get you started.

To begin, there are many notable differences between county jails of early times and state-run or privately-run prisons today. County jails were run locally. Detainees were meant only to stay for short periods of time, such as days or weeks. They were held together whatever the charge, age, or gender; and sometimes entire families were held in cases of debt (*in 1777, John Howard called for a separation of detainees by category: criminal, gender, etc.*). In contrast with modern times, the detainees (who may have been runaway slaves, debtees, or vagrants, etc.) were not used as a workforce for private agencies, and were not used for scientific research. Forced labour and in some cases hard labour, however, has been practiced for some time since the early days. In either case, this indentured servitude has been part of the blend of punishments created for prisoners during their confinement (one form of punishment for prisoners in Britain, was to wear masks while walk-

Pentonville Prisoners, Exercise Yard, London, UK, 1862

ing in circles and chained to other prisoners). Most significantly, in the very early days, punishment was not the undergirding rationale for detainment in jail itself, but where people awaited to know what their punishment would be; this timeframe would have been relatively short. Today, even with the *habeas corpus* law, the wait can often be years, some of which may be spent in solitary confinement.

Today, capital punishment (legalized killing) has largely been abandoned as a consequence to crime (*first argument for proportionality vs severity was made in writing by Cesare Beccaria, 1764*). Instead, prisoners are often held or sentenced for exceedingly long periods of time: from years - to a lifetime. And, they are not held in spaces that resemble anything like the village jails from previous centuries mentioned above. Instead, massively expensive compounds have been erected today that are, in some cases, privatized to serve a profit margin alongside guidelines of state laws regarding the holding of prisoners, but are supposed to uphold the human rights natural to all people. See Office of the High Commissioner for Human Rights: *https://www.ohchr.org/en/instruments-mechanisms/instruments/basic-principles-treatment-prisoners*.

The evolution regarding modern-day prisons have been based on recognizable templates that originated from the German and Dutch workhouses:

> Reform efforts that would actually result in something approximating a modern prison, with its population restricted to convicted criminals undergoing punishment while separated from the rest of society by long-term confinement in state-run facilities, appeared toward the end of the eighteenth century. (Rubin, 2019)

The *American Revolution* (1775 - 1783) largely influenced what we colloquially recognize today as the: penal system/penitentiary/incarceration/correctional facility/detention centre. The first state prison for criminal convicts was authorized in 1785, Massachusetts, USA.

What followed, was an experiment of sorts in how to effectively and efficiently house and 'employ' the prison population. Some measures have been more disastrous than others. Solitary confinement, perhaps the most controversial of punitive measures, was initially not intended to be punitive. In the early 1800s, it was thought that isolation would provide the space and silence for the offender to self-reflect and self-reform in order to change their inclinations in line with the greater society. It was quickly realized that, in fact, this form of isolation was deprivation of what is largely determined to be a mammalian human life — socialization and interaction with the greater world, and all the biological implications that are necessary to being an effective human in terms of physiological health (today recognized as basic human rights by most, though not legalized). It was realized that the practice of solitary confinement was de-naturing and inhumane, rather than re-constructing the person for the better, and the practice fell largely out of popularity by the 1840s. In modern times, however, there have been revivals, including the *Supermax* system. For more information see: *https://www. nwac.ca/assets-knowledge-centre/NWAC-Indigenous-Women-in-Solitary-Confinement-Aug-22.pdf*

The *American Civil War* (1861-1865), the abolishment of slavery in 1865, and the outlawing of peonage in 1867, then brought further changes. During the *Reconstruction Period* (1865–1876) in the American South, plantation owners and other businessmen, realizing they needed to fill the labour gap due to the abolishment of slavery, turned to an exception in the *13th Amendment* (the abolishment of slavery), which stated that all forms of slavery were ratified as abolished "except as punishment for a crime". Between the 1870s - 1890s, this exception set into place the cultivation of a labour force throughout the prison system — a labour force for which a lessee would only have to pay a lease fee for the prisoner to the state. There were no regulations in place for care while the prisoner was leased to the lessee, and no sanctions if the prisoner was injured or died. And thus began the long history of over-incarceration based on false, exagerrated, or frivilous charges. And, beginning in 1868, convict leases were issued to private parties. This system of allowing dealings of private citizens extracting labour from incarcerated individuals ended in the early 1900s (but was replaced by private prison contracts later on).

The twentieth century brought new models of prisons. In America, the formats introduced were based on the southern slave plantations that spanned over several thousand acres. The prisoners lived in army-style barracks and were segregated based on skin colour. During the day, the people (prisoners) worked in fields, which were guarded by an *overseer*, as in the plantation days of slavery. Up until the mid-20th century, the *chain gang* had also been implemented, which was made up mostly of African Americans. These men, while chained together, wearing striped white and black uniforms, performed

Chaingangs, unknown (c.1900)

forced labour building roads, railroads, clearing land, and digging ditches, mining for coal, among other tasks, without pay. Forced labour during this period in prisons also included the manufacture of textiles, furniture and other supplies. According to the University of Chicago Law School Research Report titled *Captive Labour* (2022), this *"allowed Northern states to produce in one year alone what, in today's dollars, amounts to over $30 billion worth of prison-made goods."* And, in the South:

> Under the convict leasing system, this work was conduct-
> ed under the supervision of private employers who could
> bid on and "lease" incarcerated people for days, months, or
> years to work on plantations and at coal mines, turpentine
> farms, sawmills, phosphate pits, railways, and brickyards.
> These private employers had unfettered control over unpaid,
> predominantly Black workers and subjected them to brutal
> punishments such as whipping and branding and, in many
> cases, worked incarcerated people to death. In Mississip-
> pi, not a single leased convict lived long enough to serve a
> 10-year sentence. Because the leasing system was so profita-
> ble for Southern states and lessees alike, new laws known as
> *Black Codes* were passed which permitted sheriffs to arrest
> Black men on specious charges and indirectly allowed states
> to expand their convict leasing programs.

For more information see: *https://www.aclu.org/sites/default/files/field_doc-ument/2022-06-15-captivelaborresearchreport.pdf.* Although chain gangs have largely fallen out of favour, there are still some versions that remain.

Around this time (post *Industrial Revolution*), separate prisons for women had to be put into place: in the US (New York, NY) in 1835; in the UK (Holloway, London) in 1903; and in Canada (Kingston, Ontario) in 1913. Some used a *reformatory* model based on the social views of how women must behave; whilst others used the male *custodial* model, which mainly took over as the twentieth century unfurled.

It is important to note that all of the major changes that occurred across the aforementioned (brief and succinct) history were motivated by prison reform-ers. Prison reformers were made up of public opinion, but were also organ-ized individuals in society who weighed the utility and practices of prisons with a critical lense, and were a vital force in mitigating over-forces.

Youth in custody were a particular concern for reformists. Whilst the tide had changed towards believing that adults could change and, therefore, confinement and punishment was their lot, young people carried hope. Reformists advocated that first-time youth and young-adult offenders ought to have separate facilities in which they could learn and in a sense reform. The following websites have a condensed history of youth incarceration (*also covered briefly in Section 4 of this book*):

a) **Canada, Osgoode Hall Law Journal, York University:** *https://digitalcommons.osgoode.yorku.ca/cgi/viewcontent.cgi?referer=&httpsredir=1&article=2141&context=ohlj*

b) **Britain, Institute of Historical Research**: *https://archives.history.ac.uk/history-in-focus/welfare/articles/bradleyk.html*

c) **USA, Centre on Juvenile and Criminal Justice:** *http://www.cjcj.org/education1/juvenile-justice-history.html*

American Reformatory Superintendent, Zebulon Brockway (1827-1920), is credited as having lobbied successfully in New York to construct a separate facility. The new reformatory opened its doors in 1876, in Elmira, NY. Young inmates were given basic education, vocational training, and religon, (other excessively punitive measures were also cast). This reform system extended beyond the inmate's release as they would continue to be supervised, thus the first *parole* and *probation* systems were introduced. This system was adopted by other reformatories into the 20th century.

Of considerable note is that although Brockway is credited into the banks of history as a reformer, he was also the subject of an investigation against allegations of abuse. In Alexander Pisciotta's 1994 book, *Benevolent Repression: Social Control and the American Reformatory-prison Movement*, he writes, "*The final report of the committee, released on 14 March 1894, was unequivocal; its findings were unanimously endorsed by the ten members of the New York State Board of Charities: 'That the charges and the allegations against the general superintendent Z.R. Brockway of 'cruel, brutal, excessive, degrading and unusual punishment of the inmates' are proven and most amply sustained by the evidence, and that he is guilty of the same.'* Brockway was in his 67th year at the time of these findings, but did not retire until his 73rd, in 1900, following further criticism. Brockway was even voted Mayor in his 77th year, revealing how popular the views toward punishment of prisoners was at that time in Elmira, NY.

Between the1920s-1930s, America began building storied rectangular prisons that came to be known as the *Big House*, which were designed to hold thousands of prisoners as compared with earlier models that were only designed to hold hundreds of people. This forecast into the number of people that would eventually come to be incarcerated is chilling. Consequently, the resulting *prison sociology* became a field of study in academia.

For a brief period between the 1950s-1970s, more community-style rehabilitation (correctional) prisons were attempted with California leading the way. In this new model, it was attempted to try to rehabilitate any prisoner, youth or adult and thus, education was implemented among many other resources. Inmates took advantage of these opportunities by learning to read, write, and broaden their perspectives. And, although there have been many books written about prisons, there were also many written during this period by prisoners themselves that went on to become best-sellers. Even though some promising achievements were made, social attiudes turned once again and tougher punishments were being sought by the general public and politicians.

The 1980s (and beyond) mark a massive proliferation in new prison compounds, with thousands being built over just a few decades, along with a corresponding all-time escalation of people being sent into captivity to fill the new spaces. A series of laws regarding long sentences with less opportunity to be let out set into place the inevitable over-crowding that continues today. This over-crowding in turn warranted even more compounds to be built. The new system of prisons have developed into what is known as *Warehouses* because it is here in which people's lives are warehoused as the newest form of punishment. Along with these recent changes, *Supermax* facilities have also become commonplace in which inmates can spend years and even decades in permanent lock-down with no human contact except one hour per day. The social and psychological affects of this type of treatment are wrought with controversy and concern. It has come to the forefront that the prison system is not a well-designed system for handling human problems.

Following the definitions on the next page, there are prompts for dialogue in order to facilitate thinking more critically about these issues.

"The prison system is not just broken, it is built on a fiction. Prison doesn't work. We need to come together and imagine what does."

~ Maya Schenwar, Journalist & Author
"prison produces more prison",
TEDx Baltimore, 2016

Prison Tour, Wales, UK (1781)
Thomas Pennant (1726-1798)

Definitions:

Source: Oxford English Dictionary / www.oed.com

Abolition: the action or process of abolishing something; the fact of being abolished or done away with; suppression, destruction, annihilation; an instance of this.

Origin: Of multiple origins. Partly a borrowing from French. Partly a borrowing from Latin. Etymons: French *abolition*; Latin *abolitiōn-, abolitiō*.

Etymology: Middle French, French *abolition* action of pronouncing an offence invalid, amnesty (1405; 1316 in Old French as *abolucion* in this sense), act of destroying completely (1538) and its etymon classical Latin *abolitiōn-, abolitiō* destruction, obliteration, cancellation, annulment, withdrawal (of a charge), amnesty < *abolit-* , past participial stem of *abolēre* (see abolish v.) + -iō -ion suffix1. Compare Old Occitan *abolitio* (1424; Occitan abolicion), Catalan *abolició* (1415), Spanish *abolición* (a1255), Portuguese *abolição* (a1649), Italian *abolizione* (a1540))

Carceral: of or belonging to a prison.
Etymology: Latin *carcerālis, carcer* prison

Prison:

a. Without article, frequently preceded by a preposition, as to prison, in prison. Originally: the condition of being kept in captivity or confinement; forcible deprivation of personal liberty; imprisonment. Hence (now the usual sense): a place of incarceration (see sense 1b).

b. With article or other designation. A building or other facility to which people are legally committed as punishment for a crime or while awaiting trial.

In North America, prison denotes a facility run by the state or federal government for those who have been convicted of serious crimes, in contrast to a locally run facility for those awaiting trial or convicted of minor offences. Cf. jail n., state prison n. at state n. Compounds 3a.

Origin: A borrowing from French. Etymons: French prisoun, prison.

Etymology: Anglo-Norman prisoun, preson, presoun, presun, pressun, prisone, prisonne, prisoune, prisune, presone, Anglo-Norman and Old French prisun, prison (Middle French, French prison) action of taking prisoner (c1100), imprisonment, captivity (c1140), prisoner, captive, detainee (c1140), place of detention (c1210) < classical Latin prensiōn- , prensiō action or power of making an arrest (see prension n.). Compare post-classical Latin prisio captivity, place of captivity (late 12th cent.), seizure, imprisonment (1281, 1313 in British sources), prisona place of captivity (frequently 1200–1483 in British sources; also occasionally as priso), priso prisoner (frequently from 12th cent. in British and continental sources), prisonus, prisona (feminine) prisoner (from 13th cent. in British sources). Compare Old Occitan preisos, Italian prigione (beginning of the 13th cent. as prescione; < French), Spanish prision (c1129), Portuguese prisão (1130).

The sense 'prisoner' (which occurs in Italian and Spanish as well as in French, English, and Latin) appears to have arisen from a person taken (in war) and held as a captive, being considered as a capture (compare senses of Old French prise at prise n.2, and also prize n.1).

Penology:

1. The study of penal policy and the methods and processes used to punish crime. Its subjects include the nature, purpose, and effectiveness of punishment. See feature Punishment, Theories of. See also criminology.

2. More specifically, the study of prison management.

***

It is the writer's hope that this first section has inspired the reader to seriously consider the ideas, research further, and develop informed views on these very important issues.

The remaining sections will present some philosophical perspectives in order to inspire the reader to extend their interest further, and perhaps organize or participate in group dialogues.

Below, an image from the Pentonville Prison, London, UK (1895), where a meaningless task was given to the prisoners. They were to walk the treadmill for up to eight hours per day.

Pentonville Prison, London, UK (1895)

The following two pages
reveals information contained
on the website for the
UN Office of the High
Commissioner for Human
Rights, and is an official
document. This resolution,
regarding administrative
aspects of prison and
incarceration, was adopted
and approved by the UN
General Assembly (45th
General Session) in 1990-91.

Invisible: A Society of Prisons

VI. STAFF

15. Recruitment

15.1 There shall be no discrimination in the recruitment of staff on the grounds of race, colour, sex, age, language, religion, political or other opinion, national or social origin, property, birth or other status. The policy regarding staff recruitment should take into consideration national policies of affirmative action and reflect the diversity of the offenders to be supervised.

15.2 Persons appointed to apply non-custodial measures should be personally suitable and, whenever possible, have appropriate professional training and practical experience. Such qualifications shall be clearly specified.

15.3 To secure and retain qualified professional staff, appropriate service status, adequate salary and benefits commensurate with the nature of the work should be ensured and ample opportunities should be provided for professional growth and career development.

16. Staff training

16.1 The objective of training shall be to make clear to staff their responsibilities with regard to rehabilitating the offender, ensuring the offender's rights and protecting society. Training should also give staff an understanding of the need to co-operate in and co-ordinate activities with the agencies concerned.

16.2 Before entering duty, staff shall be given training that includes instruction on the nature of non-custodial measures, the purposes of supervision and the various modalities of the application of non-custodial measures.

16.3 After entering on duty, staff shall maintain and improve their knowledge and professional capacity by attending in-service training and refresher courses. Adequate facilities shall be made available for that purpose.

VII. VOLUNTEERS AND OTHER COMMUNITY RESOURCES

17. Public participation

17.1 Public participation should be encouraged as it is a major resource and one of the most important factors in improving ties between offenders undergoing non-custodial measures and the family and community. It should complement the efforts of the criminal justice administration.

17.2 Public participation should be regarded as an opportunity for members of the community to contribute to the protection of their society.

18. Public understanding and co-operation

18.1 Government agencies, the private sector and the general public should be encouraged to support voluntary organizations that promote non-custodial measures.

18.2 Conferences, seminars, symposia and other activities should be regularly organized to stimulate awareness of the need for public participation in the application of non-custodial measures.

18.3 All forms of the mass media should be utilized to help to create a constructive public attitude, leading to activities conducive to a broader application of non-custodial treatment and the social integration of offenders.

18.4 Every effort should be made to inform the public of the importance of its role in the implementation of non-custodial measures.

19. Volunteers

19.1 Volunteers shall be carefully screened and recruited on the basis of their aptitude for and interest in the work involved. They shall be properly trained for the specific responsibilities to be discharged by them and shall have access to support and counselling from, and the opportunity to consult with, the competent authority.

19.2 Volunteers should encourage offenders and their families to develop meaningful ties with the community and a broader sphere of contact by providing counselling and other appropriate forms of assistance according to their capacity and the offenders' needs.

19.3 Volunteers shall be insured against accident, injury and public liability when carrying out their duties. They shall be reim-

bursed for authorized expenditures incurred in the course of their work. Public recognition should be extended to them for the services they render for the well-being of the community.

VIII. RESEARCH, PLANNING, POLICY FORMULATION AND EVALUATION

20. Research and planning

20.1 As an essential aspect of the planning process, efforts should be made to involve both public and private bodies in the organization and promotion of research on the non-custodial treatment of offenders.

20.2 Research on the problems that confront clients, practitioners, the community and policy makers should be carried out on a regular basis.

20.3 Research and information mechanisms should be built into the criminal justice system for the collection and analysis of data and statistics on the implementation of non-custodial treatment for offenders.

21. Policy formulation and programme development

21.1 Programmes for non-custodial measures should be systematically planned and implemented as an integral part of the criminal justice system within the national development process.

21.2 Regular evaluations should be carried out with a view to implementing non-custodial measures more effectively.

21.3 Periodic reviews should be conducted to assess the objectives, functioning and effectiveness of non-custodial measures.

22. Linkages with relevant agencies and activities

22.1 Suitable mechanisms should be evolved at various levels to facilitate the establishment of linkages between services responsible for non-custodial measures, other branches of the criminal justice system, social development and welfare agencies, both governmental and non-governmental, in such fields as health, housing, education and labour, and the mass media.

23. International co-operation

23.1 Efforts shall be made to promote scientific co-operation between countries in the field of non-institutional treatment. Research, training, technical assistance and the exchange of information among Member States on non-custodial measures should be strengthened, through the United Nations institutes for the prevention of crime and the treatment of offenders, in close collaboration with the Crime Prevention and Criminal Justice Branch of the Centre for Social Development and Humanitarian Affairs of the United Nations Secretariat.

23.2 Comparative studies and the harmonization of legislative provisions should be furthered to expand the range of non-institutional options and facilitate their application across national frontiers, in accordance with the Model Treaty on the Transfer of Supervision of Offenders Conditionally Sentenced or Conditionally Released.[83]

45/111. Basic Principles for the Treatment of Prisoners

The General Assembly,

Bearing in mind the long-standing concern of the United Nations for the humanization of criminal justice and the protection of human rights,

Bearing in mind also that sound policies of crime prevention and control are essential to viable planning for economic and social development,

Recognizing that the Standard Minimum Rules for the Treatment of Prisoners,[79] adopted by the First United Nations Congress on the Prevention of Crime and the Treatment of Offenders, are of great value and influence in the development of penal policy and practice,

---

[83] Resolution 45/119, annex.

Considering the concern of previous United Nations congresses on the prevention of crime and the treatment of offenders, regarding the obstacles of various kinds that prevent the full implementation of the Standard Minimum Rules,

Believing that the full implementation of the Standard Minimum Rules would be facilitated by the articulation of the basic principles underlying them,

Recalling resolution 10 on the status of prisoners and resolution 17 on the human rights of prisoners, adopted by the Seventh United Nations Congress on the Prevention of Crime and the Treatment of Offenders,[77]

Recalling also the statement submitted at the tenth session of the Committee on Crime Prevention and Control by Caritas Internationalis, the Commission of the Churches on International Affairs of the World Council of Churches, the International Association of Educators for World Peace, the International Council for Adult Education, the International Federation of Human Rights, the International Prisoners' Aid Association, the International Union of Students, the World Alliance of Young Men's Christian Associations and the World Council of Indigenous Peoples,[84] which are non-governmental organizations in consultative status with the Economic and Social Council, category II,

Recalling further the relevant recommendations contained in the report of the Interregional Preparatory Meeting for the Eighth United Nations Congress on the Prevention of Crime and the Treatment of Offenders on topic II, "Criminal justice policies in relation to problems of imprisonment, other penal sanctions and alternative measures",[78]

Aware that the Eighth Congress coincided with International Literacy Year, proclaimed by the General Assembly in its resolution 42/104 of 7 December 1987,

Desiring to reflect the perspective noted by the Seventh Congress, namely, that the function of the criminal justice system is to contribute to safeguarding the basic values and norms of society,

Recognizing the usefulness of drafting a declaration on the human rights of prisoners,

Affirms the Basic Principles for the Treatment of Prisoners, contained in the annex to the present resolution, and requests the Secretary-General to bring them to the attention of Member States.

68th plenary meeting
14 December 1990

ANNEX

Basic Principles for the Treatment of Prisoners

1. All prisoners shall be treated with the respect due to their inherent dignity and value as human beings.

2. There shall be no discrimination on the grounds of race, colour, sex, language, religion, political or other opinion, national or social origin, property, birth or other status.

3. It is, however, desirable to respect the religious beliefs and cultural precepts of the group to which prisoners belong, whenever local conditions so require.

4. The responsibility of prisons for the custody of prisoners and for the protection of society against crime shall be discharged in keeping with a State's other social objectives and its fundamental respon-

---

[84] See E/AC.57/1988/NGO/3.

sibilities for promoting the well-being and development of all members of society.

5. Except for those limitations that are demonstrably necessitated by the fact of incarceration, all prisoners shall retain the human rights and fundamental freedoms set out in the Universal Declaration of Human Rights[5] and, where the State concerned is a party, the International Covenant on Economic, Social and Cultural Rights[33] and the International Covenant on Civil and Political Rights and the Optional Protocol thereto,[33] as well as such other rights as are set out in other United Nations covenants.

6. All prisoners shall have the right to take part in cultural activities and education aimed at the full development of the human personality.

7. Efforts addressed to the abolition of solitary confinement as a punishment, or to the restriction of its use, should be undertaken and encouraged.

8. Conditions shall be created enabling prisoners to undertake meaningful remunerated employment which will facilitate their reintegration into the country's labour market and permit them to contribute to their own financial support and to that of their families.

9. Prisoners shall have access to the health services available in the country without discrimination on the grounds of their legal situation.

10. With the participation and help of the community and social institution, and with due regard to the interests of victims, favourable conditions shall be created for the reintegration of the ex-prisoner into society under the best possible conditions.

11. The above Principles shall be applied impartially.

45/112. United Nations Guidelines for the Prevention of Juvenile Delinquency (The Riyadh Guidelines)

The General Assembly,

Bearing in mind the Universal Declaration of Human Rights,[5] the International Covenant on Economic, Social and Cultural Rights[33] and the International Covenant on Civil and Political Rights,[33] as well as other international instruments pertaining to the rights and well-being of young persons, including relevant standards established by the International Labour Organisation,

Bearing in mind also the Declaration of the Rights of the Child,[85] the Convention on the Rights of the Child[52] and the United Nations Standard Minimum Rules for the Administration of Juvenile Justice (The Beijing Rules),[82]

Recalling General Assembly resolution 40/33 of 29 November 1985, by which the Assembly adopted the Beijing Rules recommended by the Seventh United Nations Congress on the Prevention of Crime and the Treatment of Offenders,

Recalling that the General Assembly, in its resolution 40/35 of 29 November 1985, called for the development of standards for the prevention of juvenile delinquency which would assist Member States in formulating and implementing specialized programmes and policies, emphasizing assistance, care and community involvement, and called upon the Economic and Social Council to report to the Eighth United Nations Congress on the Prevention of Crime and the Treatment of Offenders on the progress achieved with respect to these standards, for review and action,

Recalling also that the Economic and Social Council, in section II of its resolution 1986/10 of 21 May 1986,

---

[85] Resolution 1386 (XIV).

Dialogue Prompts:

1. Take into account that if the justice system were working, the numbers of incarcerated would not be increasing. But, even if the numbers decrease, what factors would we still need to consider to have a fair and just criminal system? How do economic, political, and social systems impact our views?

2. Does gender make a difference in how people are treated in prisons? Are prisoner human needs different from non-prisoners? What risks do female prisoners face? Male prisoners? What are the consequences to society overall when anyone is kept in captivity?

3. How did the construction of 'different races' impact the lives of people with varying skin colours? How has 'race' impacted perceived or real criminality and incarceration? What are the psychological, and overall physiological impacts on individuals and society of racializing people? How would changes in our views on 'race' impact the number of people being held in captivity?

There is little known about female incarceration and chain-gangs in the 19th Century, amidst Jim Crow laws. The following are two resources that offer more information about the lives of African-American females during this period:

Chained in Silence: Black Women and Convict Labor in the New South, by Talitha L. LeFlouria

AND

No Mercy Here: Gender, Punishment, and the Making of Jim Crow Modernity, by Sarah Haley

For more information on females in prison in the 19th Century, see: *https://brewminate.com/the-treatment-of-women-in-prison-in-the-19th-century/*

History & Definitions

"We but mirror the world. All the tendencies present in the outer world are to be found in the world of our body. If we could change ourselves, the tendencies in the world would also change. As a man changes his own nature, so does the attitude of the world change towards him. This is the divine mystery supreme. A wonderful thing it is and the source of our happiness. We need not wait to see what others do."

– Mahatma Gandhi (1869-1948)
Indian-British Lawyer & Humanist

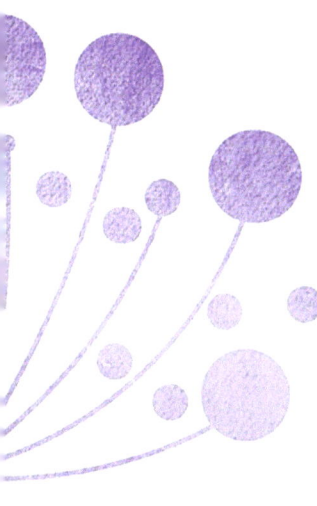

"There is only one perpetrator of evil on the planet: *human unconsciousness*. That realization is true forgiveness. With forgiveness, your victim identity dissolves, and your true power emerges – the power of Presence. Instead of blaming the darkness, you bring in the light."

–Eckhart Tolle
Spiritual Teacher & Author

St. John the Baptist in Prison.
Giovanni di Paolo (1455-1460)

"Man is not made better by being degraded."

~ *Dorothea Dix (1802-1887)*
Mental Health Advocate & Humanist

2

Philosophical Insights
Under the Surface

G iven our mysterious history of human beginnings, culture, and society — and the manufacture of prison compounds — it would be a useful exercise to step back and away, in order to take a closer look at the underlying issues that support our perspectives and consequent behaviours, through the exercise of contemplation and dialogue.

In this section, I briefly propose the following as underlying issues for critical thinking and dialogue, as well as building awareness:

i.   Human life as a force is not understood, appreciated, or embraced;

ii.   *Trauma-making* is perpetuated, due to number one;

iii. Navigating the complexity of human emotions and psychology;

iv.   Exercising vulnerability, compassion, empathy, and love.

i

Human life as a force that is not understood, appreciated, or embraced.

If you were to ask yourself, "What is *life force?*", what would you answer? Could you define it? Have you ever thought about it? Why is this an important first step in bringing awareness to complex human issues?

The *force of life* that animates humans (and other organisms: animal, plant, etc.) is a force in itself. A powerful force. It has been contemplated for millenia, but cannot be fully understood in conceptual terms. We have an intuitive sense of aliveness, especially when we turn our attention inward, but are largely without a full understanding or appreciation of it. Yet, that is *who we are* — the force itself, nature itself. This is what is spiritually referred to as *consciousness*. Without it, we would cease to physically exist in this world.

Although this force of life is who we truly are, it is not well understood or fully appreciated cognitively; yet, there is an instinctual drive to live, preserve our life, and to be safe from harm. And, this *survival instinct* is the state in which most humans largely live today. What if we became present, and considered who we *really* are, and the lives we are *really* living? Because of our suffering and struggle, it may be worthwhile to examine the conditioned manner in which we typically 'live'.

What I put forth is that, predominantly, humans are sleep-walking through life, caught in a perpetual cyle of thinking and over-thinking; driven by our thoughts and emotions, but largely unaware of how this is influencing us in dynamic ways. This is where *trauma-making* is seeded, because we have not connected with our nature, or simply put: because we are disconnected. There are severe forms of trauma, as from the extremes of psychological, sexual, emotional, and physical violence, and there are also the more common everyday ways of *trauma-making* in which we unhappily live, unaware of the real effects. We worry chronically, thinking of the past or the future, or negatively judging circumstances and people. Being alive, and truly present, here and now, is a rare occasion. Perhaps you are being brought into the present moment as you are reading or listening to these words right now. And, you may not even notice when you are taken back into the world of conditioned thinking and reacting. Or, there may even be difficulty just fully focusing on these words. The main point I am making is that we are largely unaware of the greater power within us and, thereby, underappreciate by far the actual wonder of our life itself... our life, itself, without perpetual thinking.

Though this topic is larger than the scope of this book, taking the time to look further into how truly appreciating the *life force* within us affects our attitudes and choices (as well as impacting the life of others) is imperative. Ask yourself how connecting with yourself feels, or more accurately, just being.

ii
The manner in which trauma is perpetuated, due to number one above.

Common sense informs us that trauma-perpetuates-trauma, and that people who are harmed often harm. Yet, we also rely on an intuition that informs us that this is not right: a person who has been traumatized or harmed is not entitled to traumatize or harm others. And, whether we harm — or exercise conscious control — depends on our level of awareness. But, specifically, in my view, it depends on how *critically aware* we are of our own conditioning, motivations, and behaviours, and how willing we are to challenge them.

The manner, therefore, in which trauma-making is or is not perpetuated is two-fold: 1) trauma affects our lives in a way that we are not completely aware; and because of the way we interpret and process that trauma (which has a great impact on our physiology), we may respond to that trauma in ways that are not always beneficial to ourself or another; and 2) because we *intuitively* know that it is wrong to harm others if we have been harmed, then dealing with the trauma in more informed ways ought to become a foremost priority. In this way, we are all offenders and victims of trauma-making. Some of our offences are considered illegal crimes, whilst we all communicate and interact universally in playimg a part in impacting individual experiences and societal outcomes.

Think of comparing transgressions that have different long-range impacts, e.g. *a murder* vs *a bicyle theft*. What are the differences? The chain of events pertaining to each? Given these, is it possible to really account for all the countless variables to one incident? Where do we draw the line? If we could at least consider the concept of infinite variables, we may have a broader view of why people behave the way they do. It is a matter beyond moral rules of conduct — are we really *solely* responsible for anything, and if so, to what is the reasonable and sensible degree of responsibility?

Pausing and examining the various factors that create trauma, and their meaningfulness, is helpful. The manner in which trauma-making is perpetrated then does not leave anyone out, regardless of proximity (though not everyone may bear culpable responsibility). One of the questions we could start with is '*why are we averse to considering multiple-extending-variables that contribute to outcomes?*' We may believe that choices are based strictly on personality/character, but that does not intuitively sit right, does it?

'The Death of Socrates', in prison, by
Charles Alphonse Dufresnoy, circa 1650

iii
Navigating the complexity of human emotions and mental well-being.

It is difficult enough to live as humans not understanding and appreciating the fundamental level of who we are, let alone to navigate the complexity of emotions and the psyche, and how these affect our level of awareness. But, the process of navigating this inner expanse — however haphazardly — is what we do anyway, initiated by the experiences across our life. Some of us may have had a really good start in life with kind, loving parents, security in where we lived, and healthy bonds with the people around us; whilst at the same time, for many of us, it is the opposite, or still circumstances somewhere in-between. All of these factors in circumstance play a crucial role. And so, we tend to make our way through, being acutely aware of the acceptance of others and how that can affect our own sense of value based on our circumstance vs our true being — and all of this needs healing and redirection.

I believe, as difficult as it is, that navigating the deep world of our emotions is an essential priority of being human. Because emotions have such an incredible and vast impact on our health — physical and mental — gaining awareness of them is, in my view, vital. Emotions have the power to influence our thoughts and beliefs, as well as send a cascade of chemicals and hormones through our body, which can have long-lasting impacts. Many chronic illnesses, as one example, not only have their basis in levels of stress, but research shows that healing can also take place by regulating those exacerbated emotions through mindful awareness. Due to the sheer power and force of emotions, it is worth looking further into our power to 'manufacture' healthy emotions in order to impact our attitudes and beliefs.

Neuroscience is leading the edge of discoveries in the area of our inner workings. The pre-frontal cortex of the human brain, for example, is a highly-sophisticated part of our anatomy, referred to as the *executive centre*. It is in charge of decision-making and long-term planning, and is easily impacted by elevated levels of stress, interferring with attention and focus and, ultimately, behaviour. Just one example of particular note is how the fetus' brain in eutero is affected by the level of the Mother's stress, which impacts later development in the child (*e.g. ADHD (attention-deficit hyperactivity disorder)*). Simply, stress has long-term consequences.

Amazingly, the field of neuroscience reveals that the brain is not only *plastic* — that it changes due to the inner and outer environment of the organism (e.g. thoughts, or music, and sounds) — but, that it is also *changeable* due to the choices that we make. Although the field of neuroscience is specific, it also influences a wide-range of other disciplines such as chiropractic and psychology. For further infromation, look into the wide-ranging work of *Michael Merzenich, Norman Doidge*; and *Joe Dispenza (whose work is based on the healing power of emotions)*, to name just a few. Just imagine what actively applying, indeed 'rewiring awareness' can do!

> "If our social justice is guided by retribution,
> we will simply perpetuate the use and abuse of
> power to inflict violence."
>
> ~ *Jamie Arpin-Ricci*
> *Author & Humanist*

iv
Exercising vulnerability, compassion, empathy, and love.

Love is the fundamental driving force that gives us the fuel we need to have a satisfying life. It may not seem possible, given the violent history of humans and the way we continue to live today, so let me explain my view.

When you think of what motivates you to get up in the morning, is it a feeling and attitude that is negative or positive (*remembering that feelings and attitudes are interlinked*)? If you are not sure, what is your best guess? We know, either intuitively or by experience, that a positive feeling and attitude gives us far more energy than when we feel down in our thoughts and emotions. Building greater awareness in this area can give us power over the day.

But, how does *vulnerability* play into positive emotions so that we can create more of them, and does that enable us with 'real' power?

What I am putting forth is that it is only in the space of vulnerability that we are truly able to capture the real power of love and life, and experience life in the fullest. For if we do not allow for vulnerability then we are susceptable to being walled off from the world around us, which ultimately hurts, and is not loving even to ourselves. It is possible, I am proposing, that one live with wisdom — and know who to steer clear from, and what is a dangerous versus safe situation — by remaining open *and* without barracading behind a wall of negative energy.

What I mean by energy *is* emotion.
Energy = Emotion

And, even though most of our communication (information) is non-verbal, the *emotion* we are feeling (whether we are aware of it or not), and embodying and experiencing, is the message we are sending to the world around us. Just a note, that the research varies just how much of our communication is non-verbal, from 55% - 93%. I believe it is context dependent, but that 99% of the time, non-verbal dominates by a large margin. This, I believe, is because we are instinctual creatures first and foremost, with language and advanced cognitive abilities evolving much later. We have always had to rely on our instincts (intuition) and we still do. But, unfortunately, in a highly-cognitive and analytical era, words often seem to matter more than emotions. So, the wise addage *actions speak louder than words* is an apt response to anyone espousing the lack of importance of emotions, in my view — because emotions will always drive behaviour. What has your experience been?

Imagine what life would be like without emotion — without that empowering energy — we would lose the will to live. Because emotion is a powerful *force of life energy*, we must tend to the most harmonious states, not only to survive, but to thrive as we are intended to. Are we brave enough to love?

For these reasons, I suggest that the finest of feelings: *compassion, empathy,* and *love*, are worth developing and sustaining. The power behind these emotions make life beautiful and a wonder out of the world. In this state, we are able to *feel the life force* in us because we are not taken over by negative thinking, worry and fear. In this state, we can recognize that it is only a sense of disconnect that carries us away from our true self. And, the more connected we are within, the less we are desirous of blaming and punishing others. In this way, we can see the value of and make a space for real life to be experienced. It begins by allowing.

The perspectives on incarcerating humans can be reviewed by considering the various complexities of human existence, and how we live in society. On the following pages are some points to examine before the dialogue prompts are presented. By all means, use these as further sources for critical thinking!

"Justice demands integrity. It's to have a moral universe — not only know what is right or wrong but to put things in perspective, weigh things. Justice is different from violence and retribution; it requires complex accounting."

~ Bell Hooks (1952-2021)
Author & Humanist

1. What does *prevention* of transgressions look like? What is society's part in preventing transgressions, and what does it look like?

2. Considering the lives of children, is it just when children (as young as ten) and teens are being sentenced as adults?

3. What about the sick, elderly, and dying — is there room for mercy? Do two wrongs make a right — and is that the foundation of a just and humane society?

4. Is everyone who is not in prison of *high moral* character? Administrators?

5. How could it be argued that prison staff must be trained and tested in high-moral fortitude if rehabilitation is the true purpose of prisons?

6. What is the true purpose of prisons? Retribution? Responsibility? Rehabilitation? House of correction? Warehouse for sentient lives? Is the human physiology taken well into consideration? Consider that it is not possible to make someone well and moral whilst making them mentally, emotionally, and physically ill. Are arguments for prisons sound? What are the real outcomes?

7. Do we really want vengence? Is there a lack of love that our own hearts are deprived of by not sufficiently nurturing ourselves and others?

8. Why is it that some seek gory entertainment as a kind of perverse pleasure to the senses, yet openly abhor the most minor transgressions as they perceive them to be?

9. How much are you willing to pay to hold people behind bars? The current average cost to hold an adult male in a Canadian prison is $115,000/male; and $175,000/female. That is 3-5 times more than the average person makes in wages per year. What is the real cost/benefit to individuals and society?

10. Would we perceive differently, respond differently, or with more compassion, if we knew, understood, and appreciated the *true value* of human life?

11. How does the lack of communities — and urban living — contribute to increased crime rates? How would re-allocating prison funds affect this?

12. How might people 'on the outside' take social responsibility for creating harmonious and empathic communities, based on understanding; and, instilling proper quality education, housing, food, and mental and physical care?

13. How might administrators and politicians take responsibility for the crime environment they construct through the setting of various laws and policies?

"In addition to this 'educational purpose', punishment has another socio-psychological function... Punishing the criminal provides a form of gratification for the aggressive and sadistic drives of the masses, which are thereby compensated for the many renunciations forced upon them. Punishment makes it possible for them to transfer their aggression against the oppressive and ruling class onto the criminal, and thereby to find release for this aggression."

~ Erich Fromm (1900-1980)
Humanist Philosopher, Psychologist

Indeed, we are in this together! Whether it be teachers, judges, employers, or neighbours, our opportunity to contribute meaningfully is beyond the real impact of socially constructed preferences for skin-colour, economic status, and even aesthetics, and personalities. Our individual dominion to create a healthy society is so full of potential that the real tragedy is overlooking this.

There is no moment like the present to expand awareness, to utilize emotions for creativity, and to set your footprint into the story of humanity as one who made a difference, by allowing yourself to truly feel the full power of life.

Dialogue Prompts:

1. What is your opinion about how humans live today (surrounded by an influx of technology) and your knowledge of how humans might have lived across millennia? What are the pros and cons? Are we disconnected from our nature (external and internal)? If so, what is the real impact?

2. What is your philosophy on how we *ought* to live as humans surrounded by an abundant natural world? How are we to reconnect with our true inner nature? What is the real and significant impact of doing so?

3.. What makes some humans believe that it is okay to contain a life force behind bars? That is, to contain a *force of life* (which they did not design) within a confined jurisdiction (a prison) because it is not, as they perceive, the ideal life? Are their reasons sound? How is blame and punishment interwoven into society to produce these outcomes?

4. If you were to write a philosophy paper on justice, what would it contain? What arguments would you make? And how would you support that they are indeed sound and rational?

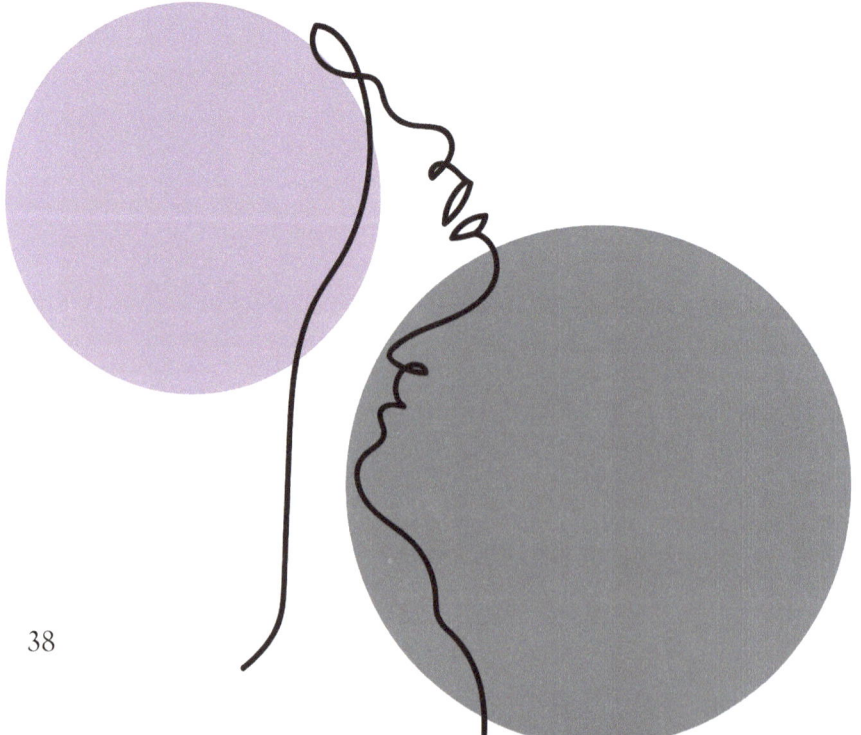

"When you see something that is not right, not fair, not just, you have to speak up. You have to say something; you have to do something."

*~ **John Lewis (1940-2020)***
Civil Rights Activist & Humanist

"Hence, we see that both statistics and the conclusions of leading experts of criminal justice confirm the fact that punishment is an almost complete failure as an effective measure for reform and correction of the criminal, deterrence, and societal security...

If, however, things are such that both today's criminal justice system and the penal system itself are ineffective, and if their own goals cannot be attained, then there must be other reasons as to why society holds on to these ineffective measures with so much determination.

Only from an examination of these motives is one led to consider that the criminal justice system has not only the actual criminal as its object, nor only the person who, although with a clean record, might become a criminal unless deterred by example, *i.e. the potential criminal...* Rather, one of the essential functions of the criminal justice system is its significance for the great mass of non-criminals."

– *Erich Fromm (1900-1980)*
Humanist Philosopher & Psychologist

"The good news is that human beings can regain their connection to themselves. Just like we can regain our sense of connection to our nature and empathy, which is a genuine human quality in us.

We are actually wired for empathy. Even rats are wired for empathy. When you stress rats in the laboratory by shocking their feet with electricity, they are more stressed when they watch other rats being shocked than when they are shocked themselves — their stress levels are higher. That's also our nature as human beings.

Contrary to the myths in our culture that we are a separate individual, aggressive, competitive creatures, we are actually wired for empathy, wired for connection, love, and compassion.

So, really to move forward, all we have to do (not an easy task, but is certainly available to us) is to get back to our true nature."

– Gabor Mate
Humanist & Author

Debtor's Prison, by Paul Gavarni.

"Prisons do not disappear social problems, they disappear human beings. Homelessness, unemployment, drug addiction, mental illness, and illiteracy are only a few of the problems that disappear from public view when human beings contending with them are relegated to cages."

~ *Angela Y. Davis*
Political Activist & Humanist

3

Real-Life Stories
Lost Lives

I t may be difficult to think about what it would be like to live for years in a prison cell — a cage built for humans; but, it may be worth while to consider how our decisions are really affecting individual lives. Perhaps you know someone who has been in or is in prison right now. Perhaps this person is a friend or family member. Or, maybe, someone in your family will one day be in prison. What are the conditions really like? What purpose does prison incarceration really serve?

There are many questions to be contemplated in order to develop a critical opinion on the matters of the criminal justice system itself, and also the manner in which humans deal with social issues. Some questions to consider are: what are appropriate responses to disruptive, threatening, or violent behaviour? Have we truly considered all the variables to those answers?

As a society, we rely on learned individuals (lawyers, politicians, and others) to think critically, and implement the best remedies. Because the issues are so complex, the average person would not generally be in a ready position to respond comprehensively. Yet, in theory, it is the support of the average person — the "public" — that the learned rely upon when laws and decisions are made. But, is it a fair and appropriate attribution to rest making those decisions on the support of a public that is not informed enough to adequately respond to such complex issues?

The following section presents various real-life stories that prompt discussion opportunities. Take different angles when considering what the average person (member of the public) may not be taking when holding a point of view regarding incarceration. Take your time to review not only the many variables to consider (biology, blame and punishment practices, religious doctrine, morals and ethics, political authority, lables and categories, family, economic, social circumstances, and rehabilitation, etc.), but also the manner in which they all inter-relate and impact individuals and society as a whole.

Billie G. McCune (1929-2007)

Source: Conversations with the Dead, by Danny Lyon

Billie spent nearly his entire life behind bars, which had begun in the early 1950s after a conviction for rape. He was sentenced to death, but it was later commuted (reduced) to a life sentence. In the book by photographer, Danny Lyon, *Conversations with the Dead*, Billie shares his hopes that the readers will consider the *"heartbreak, the loneliness, the hopes that are suppressed, the fears and doubts, the hundreds of problems both emotional and physical"* when judging those who are surviving behind bars often for years, and sometimes a lifetime.

It is not to be overlooked that while Billie was on death row (prior to his sentence being commuted), he had dismembered himself at the base of his penis. Self-mutulation whilst in prison is not uncommon, and may not be difficult to understand due to the severity of anxiety-driving conditions that people have to survive in. In this case, consider whether it is the prisoner or the system that constructs and inhabits dysfunctions that create violent outcomes?

The question looms: is our society a forgiving society? Or, does the brutality that occurs out of sight simply reassure that justice is being served? Are members of society willing to accept that a neighbour, friend, or family member may be forgotten due to our lack of active participation in the rights of humans captive behind bars? Are we satisfied that the cycle of violence perpetuated within the carceral system renders it such that a person, once caught up in the system, is likely to never gets a real opportunity for redemption for their transgressions (or in the case of the wrongfully convicted, the judgement) from society?

"My work with the poor and the incarcerated has persuaded me that the opposite of poverty is not wealth; the opposite of poverty is justice."

~ *Bryan Stevenson*
Author, "Just Mercy"

Name	McCUNE, Billie George	(W)		TPS# 122054	
True Name	Billie George McCune	Interviewed Date 2-18-53	By	HLS:mrj	

Alias	None reported	Court	District	County	Tarrant
		Offense	Rape (1)		
Date of Birth	5-8-29 Age 22				
Race	White	Sentence	Life (commuted from DEATH)		
Nativity	Waco, Texas	Sentenced	3-6-52	To Begin	3-6-52
Citizenship	United States	Plea	No	Admitted	3-6-52
Marital Status	Single	Min Exp		Max Exp	Death
Residence (Legal)	Fort Worth, Texas	Detainers	None reported		
Co-Defendants	None reported				

I. PREVIOUS CRIMNIAL HISTORY   (PRISONER'S VERSION AND DPS REPORT)
The DPS and FBI Reports show no previous arrests; however, the Subject reports several arrests for drinking and two Navy brig terms, one for drinking and simple assault and one for drinking. He states that sometime in October, 1949 in Waco, Texas he was arrested by the Police Department for being drunk. He paid a $10.00 fine. He reports that on December 1, 1949 he was arrested by the Police Department of Waco, Texas for being drunk. He served a 10 day jail sentence.

II. PRESENT OFFENSE: A. OFFICIAL VERSION: Not received.

B. PRISONER'S VERSION: The Subject states that on February 2, 1950 he arrived at Fort Worth, Texas. He states that he went to all of the industries seeking employment. He states that he was always turned down because he did not have a skill. He states that he had about $5.00 when he arrived in Fort Worth. He states that he was able to pick up enough money to live on by finding odd jobs as a porter in beer taverns and as a common laborer. On two or three occasions, when he was broke and without a job, he admits breaking into parking meters in order to get money. During this time he states that he was drinking a lot of beer and liquor. The Subject will not discuss the offense for which he was convicted. He appeared to be irrational when this was mentioned.

Correspondence received from the Austin State School, Austin, Texas reports that the Subject was received there on June 14, 1944, having been adjudicated as FEEBLEMINDED in McLennan County Court, Waco, Texas. On August 5, 1946 he was diagnosed as a normal boy with an I.Q. of 87 and transferred to the Mexia State School, Mexia, Texas. He is not reported as having committed any major infractions of the rules.

"Our problems stem from acceptance of this filthy rotten system."

~ Dorothy Day (1897-1980)
American Journalist & Humanist

B.E.S. (as per court documents)

Source: CBC Radio, As it Happens 2018

The following story is about a youth whilst in probational custody. It is important to share because of the manner in which adults interact with youth and specifically, the risk to children within the adult criminal system. Moreover, this story speaks to the dysfunction and criminality that continues to occur within the prison system that is supposedly (in concept) a compound that is free of crime. It is important to consider whether it makes sense that society allow a system that is supposed to punish and rehabilitate criminals for criminal behaviour, often contributes to (and even encourages) crime itself.

Notice: *the following real story contains graphic details about the sexual assault of a teenaged child.*

The adult survivor, who chose to remain anonymous, was interviewed by the Canadian Broadcast Corporation (CBC) in 2018 to share the details of what happend to him whilst he was a youth in governmental custody in the 1970s.

Decades after the sexual assault of a boy (B.E.S.), who was just 13-14 years old during a tour of an adult male prison (as part of the *Scared Straight* program in the 1970s) said that he is still reminded of the events of the assualt on a daily basis.

He recalled that when he was a child, he was ordered by a judge to take part in the program that was designed to scare juveniles who have commited an offence from committing crimes in the future. He was taken by a probation officer to *Oakalla Prison*, which was then located in Burnaby, BC Canada. The probation officer in charge of him handed him over to a prison guard, who then took the young boy inside the prison walls. B.E.S. recalls that he saw five men standing near a cell, and that he was pushed by the guard into the cell where the men brutally raped him while the prison guard watched and laughed at the gate.

Afterward, the guard took B.E.S. to another cell and locked him in for a long period of time. Eventually, he was taken to the front gates of the prison where the probation officer was waiting to pick him up.

B.E.S. shared how his mother noticed there was something very different about him, and took him to see a psychologist.

Although the BC government has been ordered to pay restitution to B.E.S., he said, *"I'm in my own little prison myself, and I will be for life."*

◆

"Prison creates Monsters out of People."

~ Bianca Mercer,
Peer Educator

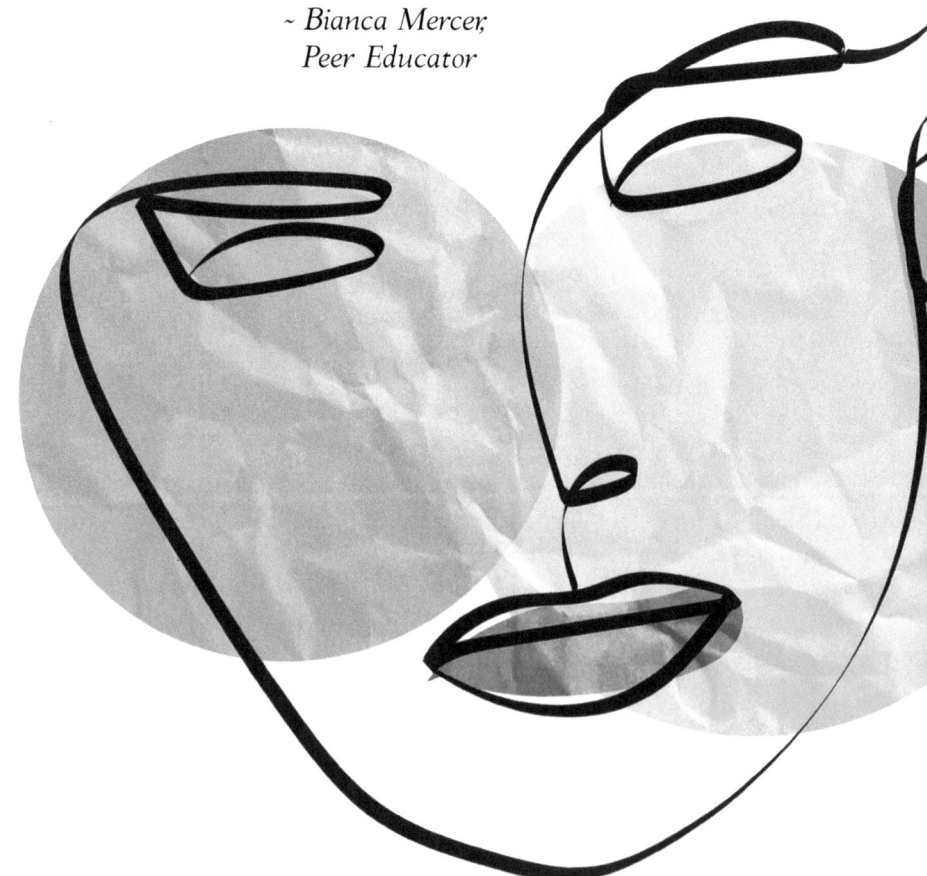

Stories of 3 Pregnant Women

Source: The Deep Magazine, 2019

The following three females were incarcerated at three different facilities respectively: the first (Bianca Mercer) at *Central Nova Scotia Correctional Facility*, known as *Burnside Jail*; the second (Julia Bilotta) at the *Ottawa-Carleton Detention Centre*; and the third female (Unnamed) at the federal *Nova Institution for Women*, known as *Nova* in Truro, Nova Scotia, at the time of these incidents.

"There is one mother-and-baby program at the Nova Institution for Women, but this kind of program doesn't exist in provincial jails, where women convicted of lesser crimes such as drug possession, sex trafficking, and theft serve their sentences, or await trial during long stints on remand—sometimes months long." ~ Maggie Rahr, *The Deep* magazine

Bianca Mercer

Source: The Deep Magazine, 2019

Bianca's story of how she got caught in the cycle of incarceration is like that of many. She describes her early childhood with a physically abusive Mother, and not having known her real Father. She has been in and out of foster care and has experienced homelessness as a child. After getting involved with other desperate people living hard lives on the streets, Bianca became pregnant. By 20, she was addicted to drugs, and her son was removed at just 13 months-old into the custody of Child Welfare Services.

Bianca was consumed by grief over the removal of her son, and dove into drugs, and consequently sexwork to support her habit. *"I was strictly using to take away the feelings I was trying to ignore."* Charges for theft, fraud, drug-trafficking, and more followed, along with being held in jail awaiting trial beginning in 2015. *"Bianca was one of the 62 percent of inmates held on remand at Burnside, who haven't yet had a trial. They're just there, waiting. Overall, 57 percent of prisoners in Nova Scotia provincial jails are awaiting trial, making the province one of seven provinces and territories where more prisoners are in jail on remand than in sentenced custody (In 2015-16, Alberta had the highest remand rate, at 70 percent.)".*

After a prenatal visit, Bianca's doctor advised that she needed to relax and stay calm as the amniotic fluid surrounding the baby was not optimal. In spite of this and common sense, the guards put her into solitary confinement, leaving the fluorescent lights on; and, due to this Bianca could not know how much time had passed or what day it was, negatively affecting her and her baby's circadium rhythm and overall health and well-being. After lodging a complaint, Bianca's mattress was removed. Four months pregnant, and with her baby in an insecure state, Bianca was made to lie on a concrete floor as punishment for a misdemeanour incident that occured prior to her doctor's visit. Bianca said it felt *"like forever"*, remaining in solitary confinement for seven days, only to be let out for 30 min per day, and then switched to lock down in her cell.

Bianca shared how the hostile and demeaning environment was affecting her mental health, *"I was giving up."*

Solitary confinement is supposed to be used only as a last resort, according to the Director for Correctional Services at Burnside, Sean Kelly, and a review is supposed to take place for any person held in such conditions for more than 24 hours. But, Bianca says that never happened in her case. *"I'm not suggesting there aren't times where their rights are violated,"* said Kelly.

Bianca was nearing full term when she was released with the help of the *Elizabeth Fry Society* workers. But, her baby died in utero. The only explanation Bianca received from her doctors was that her baby, whom she named Althea Layton Lynn Israel, was under duress.

Bianca had already lost a son, which she numbed by taking drugs and that eventually landed her behind bars. But, this time Bianca was sober: *"I'm moving forward with that memory permanently stuck inside my mind for the rest of my life."*

Julie Bilotta

Source: *The Deep Magazine, 2019*

In 2012, Julie went into labour at the *Ottawa-Carleton Detention Centre* in a confinement cell. Guards refused to take Julie's labour pains seriously even after the baby's foot began to make an appearance whereafter Julie was asked by a guard whether the baby was contraband. After ten minutes, another foot entered the world — the delivery was breach — but, it was not until twenty minutes later that an ambulance was called. And, another 30 minutes would pass before paramedics would arrive. The baby was born onto a cold concrete floor, one month premature, with the umbilical cord wrapped around his tiny neck.

It was only in the ambulance that Julie could hold her baby, but then he was removed from her for a further three weeks.

The *College of Nurses of Ontario* confirmed the details in a 2014 disciplinary decision, which was made public.

The tragic ending to this heartbreaking story, which could have been prevented under a more evolved and humane social system, is that little Gionni Lee died shortly after his first birthday after suffering from respiratory complications.

Julie filed a lawsuit, which is currently pending (as of this publication).

Although this case was met with public outrage, incarcerating Mothers is still a common practice in Canada.

Unamed Woman with Mental Health Impairment
Source: The Deep Magazine, 2019

In autumn 2014, an *Elizabeth Fry* volunteer, who would visit women in prisons and observe conditions, noticed that there was one woman who would never join in the sessions. Eventually, the volunteer convinced the dishevelled woman to join in, but was perplexed by her overall condition. The woman was clearly pregnant, but because of her impression, the volunteer wondered how this could ever have happened in the first place.

Martha Paynter, founder of *Women's Wellness Within*, an organization that advocates for and supports female inmates, was made aware of the case. It was learned that the woman had been in provincial care for most of her life, and had mental health issues, and a lower cognition than is typical for her age, and it was unclear how the woman got pregnant. Paynter was very concerned what could happen once the woman went into labour. *"If we don't get in there,*" she said firmly, "she'll have a psychotic break."

The process of getting help for the woman in cusstody was so arduous that support for her care and delivery of her baby was not permitted inside the prison. Paynter's prediction, and worst fear, evenutally came to pass.

The woman's labour was described as nothing short of intense and chilling. Guards who witnessed the birth described it as though watching a caged animal that was being attacked. The baby was taken into provincial care immediately.

The woman was taken to *Colchester East Hants Health Centre*, and eventually to a psychiatric institution in Quebec, where she remains.

Some of the witnesses to the birth had to take a stress leave due to the trauma of having experienced such a horrifying scene.

According to *Canada's Office of the Correctional Investigator,* the number of women federally incarcerated increased by 40% between 2006-2016, the majority of whom are Mothers. Not only is the fastest growing population of those incarcerated in Canada women, but one-third are Aboriginal women, and their incarceration rate has increased by 109%.

For more information see:

https://www.nwac.ca/assets-knowledge-centre/NWAC-Indigenous-Women-in-Solitary-Confinement-Aug-22.pdf

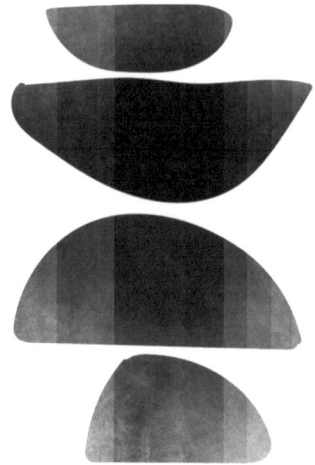

"If one really wishes to know how justice is administered in a country, one does not question the policemen, the lawyers, the judges, or the protected members of the middle class. One goes to the unprotected — those, precisely, who need the law's protection most! — and listens to their testimony."

~ *James Baldwin (1924-1987)*
American Author & Humanist

"Overcoming poverty is not a gesture of charity. It is an act of justice. It is the protection of a fundamental human right, the right to dignity and a decent life."

~ Nelson Mandela (1918-2013)
Former South African President & Humanist

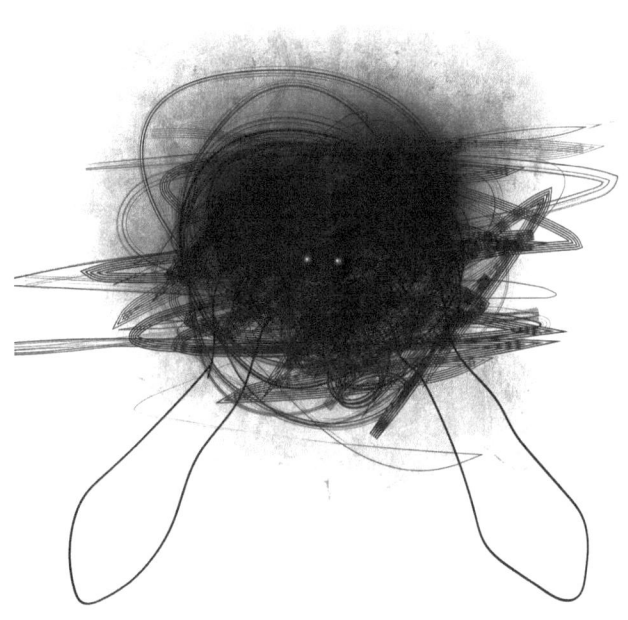

Guard, Oakalla Prison-1970s-Burnaby, BC Canada

Main Entrance, The Walls-Danny Lyons-1967-68-Ellis Prison Texas

Shake Down-Danny Lyons-1967-68-Ellis Prison Texas

Building Shake Down-Danny Lyons-1967-68-Ellis Prison Texas

Oakalla Prison-1970s-Burnaby, BC Canada

Cell-Oakalla Prison-1970s-Burnaby, BC Canada

Youth Incarceration

The Mother-Child Bond is innate and life-long (*which may be affected if she is experiencing extreme mental health issues*). Her physiological well-being and its affect on her child are commonly accepted, but little is known about how the child's state affects the Mother. Relatively few studies have shown that Mothers' health is negatively impacted when her child (whether boy or girl) is either stopped by police, held captive, or is incarcerated long-term.

The following are a series of abstract excerpts from some articles published that address the health affects of incarceration on the Mother and other family members, and which have long term generational consequences.

The Strain of Sons' Incarceration on Mothers' Health (2020). *Abstract:* Research on disadvantage across generations typically focuses on the resources that parents pass on to their children. Yet, social disadvantage might also result from the transmission of adverse experiences from children to their parents. This paper explores one such adverse experience by examining the influence of a son's incarceration on his mother's health. Using panel data from the 1979 National Longitudinal Survey of Youth and its young adult follow up (n=2,651 mothers; 18,390 observations), the paper shows that mothers are more likely to suffer health limitations after a son is incarcerated. A time-distributed fixed effects analysis indicates that the effect on maternal health may persist or even grow over time. Rather than a short-term shock whose effect soon diminishes, a son's incarceration is a long-term strain on mothers' health. The disproportionate incarceration of young men in disadvantaged communities is thus likely to contribute to cumulative adversity among mothers already at risk of severe hardship. More broadly, the results suggest how children's adverse experiences may influence parental well-being, producing further disadvantage across generations.

For more information see:
https://www.campaignforyouthjustice.org/news/blog/item/stories-from-mothers-of-incarcerated-youth

Women's health in the era of mass incarceration (2021). *Abstract*: Dramatic increases in criminal justice contact in the United States have rendered prison and jail incarceration common for US men and their loved ones, with possible implications for women's health. This review provides the most expansive critical discussion of research on family member incarceration and women's health in five stages.

Assessing mass incarceration's effects on families (2021). *Abstract*: In this Review, we assess how mass incarceration, a monumental American policy experiment, has affected families over the past five decades. We reach four conclusions. First, family member incarceration is now common for American families. Second, individuals who will eventually have a family member incarcerated are worse off than those who never will, even before the incarceration takes place. Third, family member incarceration has negative effects on families above and beyond these preexisting disadvantages. And finally, policy interventions that address the precursors to family member incarceration and seek to minimize family member incarceration would best enhance family well-being. If the goal is to help all American families thrive, then the importance of simultaneous changes in social and criminal justice policy cannot be overstated.

Mothers' health following youth police stops (2021). *Abstract*: In the present study, we examined the association between youth police stops and mothers' health. We used data from the Fragile Families and Child Wellbeing Study, a cohort of urban children born around the turn of the 21st century and followed through adolescence (2014 to 2017), to estimate the association between youth police stops and mothers' health (measured by overall health and health limitations). Analyses reveal that youth police stops had deleterious repercussions for mothers' health, net of their health prior to the stop. These health consequences emerged regardless of the frequency or intrusiveness of the stop. The negative association between youth police stops and overall health was larger among mothers of girls than among mothers of boys. Associations were similar across mothers' race/ethnicity and education. Taken together, results show that youth police stops exacerbate health problems among mothers. Given the concentration of police stops among youth of color, these findings highlight the consequences of the criminal justice system for population health inequalities.

Vicarious exposure to the criminal legal system among parents and siblings (2022). *Introduction:* The growth of the criminal legal system in recent years has extended the reach of carceral surveillance, control, and punishment into the lives of families and produced staggering disparities in familial connectedness to the system. The disproportionate risks of arrest, correctional supervision, and incarceration among poor young Black boys and men, for example, mean that the family members of these young people also experience heightened levels of vicarious exposure to the system. Criminal legal system contacts have been linked to a host of negative spillover effects for family members, including strained or reduced relationship quality, increased health risks, shortened life expectancy, and declines in household economic resources. In these ways, the expansion of police surveillance and punitive punishment over the past several decades had harmful consequences both for system involved young people and for the family members who care for and about them.

***

Based on the above research studies (and much other data), it is clear that a retributive system works against the entire community by the consequential affects on family connections; has detrimental affects on the entire way humans live; and in broader terms the social, economic, and physiological well-being of everyone. The ricochet affect of a society that upholds punishment to nurture needs to be understood and reviewed seriously, so that reparative changes may begin. Jeff Wallce spoke of "habilation" instead of "re-habilitation" in his talk. It does not make logical or rational sense to re-habilitate anyone to a traumatized and toxic norm, which is largely the state of human beings world-over. If we do not see the damaged lives we are living, we are unable to allow, conceive of, or believe another, more evolved, culture can predominate. And, where unjust constructs have taken over and diminished the lives of so many, there needs to be in place sober reflection. The nurturing of individuals in society has to be brought to the table. To habilitate then means to humanize a person who has been de-humanized by simply existing in modern society with all its technological advances.

Incarcerating youth is not the answer to 'delinquency'. Adults are empowered with making decisions that affect lives, and so must take responsibility for the direction of their mindset. Put another way, adults must be contributing to cultivate a healthy society instead of continuing to believe that transgressions beget punishment. Adults need to be the role-models and heal society. It is not sustainable not to answer this call and, thereby, to make contributions that uphold violence. In a retributive society, no one is victimless. Adults need to 'grow up' — we must make healing a priority.

In this way, a greater understanding of human individual needs with an emphasis on nurture and understanding is required; especially in a society that has grown all the more impatient as technology has progressed at light speed.

The basic needs of any human, it could be plainly argued, does not need reams of research studies (though they seem to convince) in order to implement empathic attention towards one another, gentleness in approach, suspending judgement, and kindness. This basic relational method may save us all a lot of headache and trauma in the short-term and long-run, which has eventual impacts on humanity (and the earth) into the future.

***

On the matter of trauma, renowned humanist, author, and world expert on trauma, Gabor Mate, in his most recent release, *The Myth of Normal* (2022), reveals honestly the true underlying issues of why humans are living in precarious states, why we are consciously unaware for the most part, and why we emit traumatized behaviours. He reveals how important our emotional states are to our physiology and communities. Through Mate's work (and others), we can begin to piece together the not-so-puzzling reasons why children behave the way they do. It is only a natural response — though the responses vary from person to person (nature + nurture) — due to environment. And so, it is logical that we need to understand humans, not punish them. Punishing others, our children, is projecting onto them our own trauma, which needs to stop because children learn largely from what is modeled, not strictly what they are told. Let's model gentleness, understanding, calmness, patience, non-judgement, empathy, and thus, we will teach them the same through mutuality and by taking responsibility as adults. In this way, their confidence is built up, rather than torn down and 're-habilitated' to toxic, but largely ignorant, adult expectations. And, in the process we shall heal too.

Before dialogue prompts, the following are pages regarding the lived-experiences of youth who have been incarcerated. Thereafter, a letter to the US Attorney General, re: juvenile life without parole in the federal system.

Invisible: A Society of Prisons

Austin Eversole

Source: Java Films Documentary

When Austin was in his 15th year, he was tried as an adult, and sent to an adult prison in Brazoria, Texas. His was convicted for patricide (killing one's Father) after a long history of being beaten and humilated daily by his Father. He is currently serving a 40 year sentence.

In a documentary interview he reveals, "I shot him because I thought seriously that my life was in danger. And, he had already told me earlier in the day that he wanted to kill me and he had a knife near him. So, I just...I snapped. I wish I wouldn't have. Irrationally, I thought that by killing him I would end the trouble and that, I guess, my life would be good. I don't know. This is the mind of an under-developed fifteen-year-old."

Austin did not have his case heard before a court and jury. Instead, his court-appointed lawyer convinced him to sig an agreement, which would hold him captive in jail for the next 40 years.

It is not an understatement that anyone could hardly imagine the terror of being a child who has been forced by 'learned' adults, who knowingly and deliberately sent him to be housed in a prison amongst adults for the next 40 years of his life.

Austin shared, "*You're so young, and you see these people, and a lot of the time you're like, 'Oh, I want what he's got' or 'he's cool' or 'he reminds me of my Dad'. And, that puts you in the trajectory to live in a bad way, because you're not around positive people, you're surrounded by criminals, people that are hardened, people that have been doing this, y'know, time after time.*"

Austin is still serving his sentence, and is scheduled to be released in his 55th year, in 2049.

Kalief Browder

Source: Java Films Documentary

Kalief's story has been the subject of public outrage, and was also included in a documentary mini-series titled *The Kalief Browder Story* produced by famous music rapper *Jay-Z*. Kalief was in his 16th year when he was sent to *Rikers Island jail* in New York, between 2010 and 2013, of which 2 years were spent alone in a tiny windowless cell, in solitary confinement (23hrs/day). He tried to commit suicide several times. He had not yet been to trial, and had not yet been convicted. The charges stemmed from the alleged theft of a backpack.

In a 2013 interview with *The HuffPost*, after his release, Kalief shared his soulful plea that changes needed to be made: *"What they do is they starve you, they won't feed you, and it's already hard in there, because if you get three trays you're still hungry because, I guess that's part of the punishment. So if they starve you one tray that could really make an impact on you. I was starved a lot, I can't even count. This happens everyday, and I feel like this has got to stop because I feel that there's a lot of people in there for stuff that they didn't do."*

During his arduous and unforgiving term, he was taunted by other inmates for not joining a gang, arbitrarily beaten by guards, and starved. All of this erroded Kalief's mind and spirit, and in 2013, he filed a lawsuit against the New York City Police Department, the Bronx District Attorney, and the Department of Corrections. *"People tell me because I have this case against the city I'm all right. But I'm not all right. I'm messed up. I know that I might see some money from this case, but that's not going to help me mentally. I'm mentally scarred right now. That's how I feel. [There] are certain things that changed about me and they might not [change] back... Before I went to jail, I didn't know about a lot of stuff, and, now that I'm aware, I'm paranoid. I feel like I was robbed of my happiness."*

In 2015, in his 22nd year, Kalief completed his suicide at his Mother's home. The city of New York has named a street after him.

INSTITUTE FOR CONSTITUTIONAL ADVOCACY AND PROTECTION
GEORGETOWN UNIVERSITY LAW CENTER

VIA EMAIL

The Honorable Merrick B. Garland
Attorney General
U.S. Department of Justice
950 Pennsylvania Avenue NW
Washington, DC 20530

February 17, 2022

Re: Juvenile Life Without Parole in the Federal System

Dear Attorney General Garland,

We write to you as current and former federal, state, and local prosecutors, Department of Justice officials, and judges. We have extensive experience prosecuting, establishing policy for prosecuting, and seeking or imposing sentences for violent crimes, including those committed by juveniles. Based on our experience, we know that fair and proportionate punishments must account for the impact that violent crimes have on victims and survivors. Just as critically, however, we believe that the credibility of the criminal justice system requires consideration of the characteristics of juvenile offenders, including the possibility of rehabilitation.

Where a juvenile offender is capable of change—as all but the rarest will be—the Constitution and sound sentencing policy demand something less than the punishment of life without the possibility of parole. We accordingly write to urge the Department to ensure that this ultimate penalty is reserved for the rare juvenile homicide offender whose crime reflects permanent incorrigibility. Specifically, we recommend that, except in the most unusual circumstances, the Department should seek a sentence of no more than 30 years for juveniles convicted of crimes that carry a maximum sentence of life. We also recommend that the Department create a committee to review all requests by federal prosecutors to seek life sentences for juveniles, modeled on the capital case review process. The committee should also review all current cases of juveniles serving life sentences and seek sentencing reductions or commutations for those juveniles whose records establish that they are capable of rehabilitation.

We are sensitive to the pressures that the Department faces as jurisdictions across the country report increases in certain crimes, such as automobile thefts, committed by juveniles. The causes of such reported increases, and the best methods for addressing them, are complicated questions outside the scope of this letter. Our recommendations instead bear on a separate issue: just sentencing for juvenile homicide offenders. For the reasons below, we believe that life sentences will rarely be appropriate for such individuals, and that the Department should take steps to ensure consistency in the application of constitutional proportionality principles to these cases in the federal system. To the extent the Department would find it helpful, the signatories to this letter, or a subset of them, are available to discuss these recommendations further.

600 New Jersey Avenue NW, Washington, D.C. 20001 | (202) 662-9042 | reachICAP@georgetown.edu

Only the Rare, Incorrigible Juvenile Offender Should Receive the Most Severe Punishment

As prosecutors and judges, we understand that proportionality in sentencing is essential to the credibility of the criminal justice system. Our experience teaches us that even in the case of homicide—which permanently ends a person's life and forever alters the lives of others—the culpability of a juvenile is often different than that of an adult. Sentences that fail to account for these differences undermine the perception that justice has been done in a particular case, and they give the impression of unfairness on a broader scale. As Justice Frankfurter put it, "justice must satisfy the appearance of justice." *Offutt v. United States*, 348 U.S. 11, 14 (1954).

In a series of decisions spanning more than a decade, the Supreme Court has recognized that "children are constitutionally different from adults for purposes of sentencing." *Miller v. Alabama*, 567 U.S. 460, 471 (2012). Because of these differences, some sentences that may be appropriate for adults are invalid under the Eighth Amendment when imposed on juvenile offenders. In *Roper v. Simmons*, the Court held that the Eighth Amendment prohibits capital punishment for crimes committed by juveniles because "[t]he differences between juvenile and adult offenders are too marked and well understood to risk allowing a youthful person to receive the death penalty despite insufficient culpability." 543 U.S. 551, 572–73 (2005). The Court extended the logic of *Roper* in *Graham v. Florida* to bar sentences of life imprisonment without the possibility of parole for non-homicide offenses committed by juveniles. 560 U.S. 48 (2010). In doing so, the Court noted that, like a capital sentence, a sentence of life without parole "alters the offender's life by a forfeiture that is irrevocable" and that the "twice diminished moral culpability" of a juvenile non-homicide offender undermines the justification for such a severe sentence. *Id.* at 69. More recently, in *Miller v. Alabama*, as further explained in *Montgomery v. Louisiana*, the Court held that life-without-parole sentences are disproportionate for "the vast majority" of juvenile homicide offenders. 136 S. Ct. 718, 736 (2016).

These limitations on juvenile sentencing derive from the fact that, due to their "diminished culpability and greater prospects for reform," children "are less deserving of the most severe punishments." *Miller*, 567 U.S. at 471 (quoting *Graham*, 560 U.S. at 68). In particular, the Court has identified three crucial differences between children and adults for purposes of sentencing:

> First, children have a "lack of maturity and an underdeveloped sense of responsibility," leading to recklessness, impulsivity, and heedless risk-taking. Second, children "are more vulnerable . . . to negative influences and outside pressures," including from their family and peers; they have limited "control over their own environment" and lack the ability to extricate themselves from horrific, crime-producing settings. And third, a child's character is not as "well formed" as an adult's; his traits are less fixed and his actions less likely to be "evidence of irretrievable depravity."

Id. (quoting *Roper*, 543 U.S. at 569–70) (brackets and citations omitted). The Court has also emphasized the related point that a juvenile offender "might have been charged and convicted of a lesser offense if not for incompetencies associated with youth—for example, his inability to deal with police officers or prosecutors (including on a plea agreement) or his incapacity to assist his own attorneys." *Id.* at 477–78.

Considering the ways in which juveniles are different from adults, *Miller* and *Montgomery* concluded that, under the Eighth Amendment, a life sentence without the possibility of parole must be reserved for the "rare" juvenile homicide offender who "exhibits such irretrievable depravity that rehabilitation is impossible and life without parole is justified." *Montgomery*, 136 S. Ct. at 733. In other words, because adolescents' "transient rashness, proclivity for risk, and inability to assess consequences" lessen their "'moral culpability' and enhance[] the prospect that, as the years go by . . . , [their] 'deficiencies will be reformed,'" *Miller*, 567 U.S. at 472 (quoting *Graham*, 560 U.S. at 68), "a lifetime in prison is a disproportionate sentence for all but the rarest of children, those whose crimes reflect 'irreparable corruption,'" *Montgomery*, 136 S. Ct. at 726 (quoting *Roper*, 543 U.S. at 573).

The Court's recent decision in *Jones v. Mississippi* does not unsettle these well-established principles. 141 S. Ct. 1307 (2021). In *Jones*, the Court held that a sentencer is not required, as a procedural matter, to make a finding that a juvenile homicide offender is permanently incorrigible before imposing a sentence of life without parole. *See id.* at 1311, 1318–19, 1321. The Court took pains to reaffirm, however, what it understood to be "[t]he key paragraph from *Montgomery*," including the following admonition: "That *Miller* did not impose a formal factfinding requirement does not leave States free to sentence a child whose crime reflects transient immaturity to life without parole. To the contrary, *Miller* established that this punishment is disproportionate under the Eighth Amendment." *Id.* at 1315, n.2 (quoting *Montgomery*, 136 S. Ct. at 735). *Jones* indicated that where such disproportionate punishment is imposed, a juvenile homicide offender may raise an as-applied Eighth Amendment challenge. *See id.* at 1322; *see also, e.g.*, *United States v. Grant*, 9 F.4th 186, 197 (3d Cir. 2021) (where a sentencer finds a juvenile homicide offender to be corrigible, but nevertheless imposes a sentence of life without parole, "the vehicle for challenging the sentence is an as-applied Eighth Amendment claim based on disproportionality of the punishment to the crime and criminal"). And although *Jones* agreed with the respondent that "permanent incorrigibility is not an eligibility criterion akin to sanity or a lack of intellectual disability," 141 S. Ct. at 1315, the Court at no point suggested that transiently immature juveniles may be sentenced to life without parole. Such a suggestion would have been incompatible with the Court's reaffirmation of "[t]he key paragraph from *Montgomery*."

Furthermore, regardless of how one interprets *Jones*, the sparing imposition of juvenile life-without-parole sentences is required as a matter of sound sentencing policy. Justice demands that punishments accurately reflect offenders' culpability and capacity for change. And for the reasons articulated in *Roper* and its progeny—and confirmed by our experience as prosecutors and judges—these considerations generally will favor more lenient sentences for juveniles. This view is supported as well by evolving scientific understandings of child psychology and the neuroscience of adolescent development. In recent years, "studies of adolescent brain anatomy clearly indicate that regions of the brain that regulate such things as foresight, impulse control, and resistance to peer pressure" are not fully developed at age 17. Laurence Steinberg, *Should the Science of Adolescent Brain Development Inform Public Policy?*, Issues in Sci. & Tech., Spring 2012, http://issues.org/28-3/steinberg/. At that time, a child is still growing into who she will become as an adult. *See, e.g., id.* ("Adolescence . . . is a time when people are, on average, not as mature as they will be when they become adults."); Mass. Inst. Of Tech., *Brain Changes*, Young Adult Dev. Project (2008), https://hr.mit.edu/static/worklife/youngadult/brain.html ("The brain isn't fully mature . . . at 18.").

Limitations on juvenile life without parole are also necessary to mitigate severe racial disparities in our criminal justice system. It is no revelation that Americans of color are disproportionately represented in the Nation's prisons and jails. *See, e.g.*, The Sentencing Project, The Color of Justice: Racial and Ethnic Disparity in State Prisons 5 (2021). But these disparities are even more pronounced when it comes to juveniles sentenced to life without parole. At the state level, Black inmates make up 40 percent of the overall prison population, but nearly *two-thirds* of the population of juveniles serving life without parole. *See* E. Ann Carson, Bureau of Justice Statistics, U.S. Dep't of Justice, NCJ 251149, Prisoners in 2016, 25 tbl.21 (2018); John R. Mills, Anna M. Dorn & Amelia Courtney Hritz, *Juvenile Life Without Parole in Law and Practice: Chronicling the Rapid Change Underway*, 65 Am. U. L. Rev. 535, 576 tbl.4 (2016). And at the federal level, our research indicates that juvenile offenders serving life sentences are disproportionately Black, Native American, and Asian relative to the prison population as a whole.

In Most Cases, the Department Should Seek Lesser Sentences for Juveniles

Due to the abolition of parole in the federal system, seeking a sentence of life *with* the possibility of parole is not an option for the Department. *See* Sentencing Reform Act of 1984, Pub. L. No. 98-473, tit. II, ch. II, 98 Stat. 1987. For the reasons given above, however, we urge the Department to advocate for a sentence of less than life where a juvenile offender is capable of rehabilitation, as nearly all will be. An appropriate sentence of years will of course depend on the particular circumstances of the crime and the characteristics of the offender. But we maintain that in the vast majority of cases, a sentence of no more than 30 years will be a fair and proportionate punishment for a juvenile homicide offender.

It is worth noting at the outset that even a sentence of 30 years will be excessive for most juvenile homicide offenders. The median length of imprisonment for murder is 20 years for *all* adults in the federal system, and the median time served before initial release for murder is 17.5 years for *all* adults in the state systems. *See* Danielle Kaeble, Bureau of Justice Statistics, U.S. Dep't of Justice, NCJ 255662, Time Served in State Prison, 2018, 1 (2021); U.S. Sentencing Comm'n, 2019 Annual Report and Sourcebook of Federal Sentencing Statistics 64 tbl.15 (2020). The median sentence for juvenile homicide offenders should fall below these benchmarks, given that juveniles have a "diminished culpability and heightened capacity for change," *Miller*, 567 U.S. at 479.

A 30-year cap, except in rare cases of permanent incorrigibility, is consistent with a number of relevant data points from the state and federal systems. First, in the years following *Miller* and *Montgomery*, many States reconsidered the appropriate sentence length for juveniles convicted of the most serious offenses. Whereas nearly all States permitted the imposition of juvenile life-without-parole sentences at the time *Miller* was decided, roughly half have now abolished such sentences and replaced them with minimum terms of years before parole eligibility. *See* The Campaign for the Fair Sentencing of Youth, Tipping Point: A Majority of States Abandon Life-Without-Parole Sentences for Children 5 (2018); The Sentencing Project, Juvenile Life Without Parole: An Overview 3–4 (2021). These include States whose elected officials span the political spectrum—from Arkansas and Utah to Hawaii and Vermont—and the new minimums that they have enacted provide guideposts regarding proportionate sentences for the most culpable juvenile homicide offenders. Of the States that now prohibit juvenile life without parole, most have enacted minimum terms of 30 years or less.

Actual resentencing practice tells a similar story. In the three years following *Montgomery*, the number of individuals serving juvenile life-without-parole sentences in the United States fell by 60 percent, from 2,800 to 1,100, as a result of legislative reform and judicial resentencing. *See*

The Campaign for the Fair Sentencing of Youth, *supra*, at 6. Of the 1,700 individuals whose sentences have been altered, the median sentence before parole or release eligibility is 25 years. *Id.* Of course, minimum sentences before parole eligibility are not perfectly analogous to terms of years in the federal system, due to the elimination of federal parole. But we believe that a 30-year determinate sentencing cap is a close substitute for a 25-year minimum sentence before parole consideration, especially when the imposition of federal supervised release is taken into account. *See* 18 U.S.C. § 3583.

Myriad other considerations support a 30-year cap for all but the permanently incorrigible. It is well documented, for example, that criminal activity is strongly negatively correlated with age. *See, e.g.*, Marc Mauer, *Long-Term Sentences: Time to Reconsider the Scale of Punishment*, 87 UMKC L. Rev. 113, 122–23 (2018). By the time juvenile offenders reach their 40s, they have long passed the peak age of criminal involvement, and their risk of recidivism has declined significantly. *See id.* at 122; U.S. Sentencing Comm'n, The Effects of Aging on Recidivism Among Federal Offenders 11 fig.1 (2017).

Furthermore, a nominal term of years understates the degree of punishment exacted on a juvenile offender. Recent research suggests that time spent in prison decreases life expectancy, perhaps even significantly. *See* Evelyn J. Patterson, *The Dose-Response of Time Served in Prison on Mortality: New York State, 1989–2003*, 103 Am. J. Pub. Health 523 (2013) (finding that each year in prison translated into a two-year decline in life expectancy). A term of 30 years may thus reduce by an even greater amount the freedom that a juvenile offender will ever have. It is no surprise that courts have found lengthy terms of years to be functional life sentences, even where the defendant can theoretically survive his time in prison. *See, e.g.*, *State v. Zuber*, 152 A.3d 197, 201–02, 212–13 (N.J. 2017) (*Graham* and *Miller* applied to the sentences of a juvenile nonhomicide offender and a juvenile homicide offender who were ineligible for parole until ages 72 and 85, respectively); *State v. Moore*, 76 N.E.3d 1127, 1133, 1149 (Ohio 2016) (*Graham* prohibited the imposition of a sentence that rendered a juvenile nonhomicide offender ineligible for parole until age 92); *State v. Ragland*, 836 N.W.2d 107, 119, 121–22 (Iowa 2013) (*Miller* prohibited the mandatory imposition of a sentence that rendered a juvenile homicide offender ineligible for parole until age 78). And the United States Sentencing Commission has treated as a "de facto" life sentence any sentence of 470 months or longer. *See* U.S. Sentencing Comm'n, Life Sentences in the Federal System 10 (2015). The presumptive maximum sentence for juvenile homicide offenders should be significantly lower than that.

The Department Should Create a Committee to Review All Requests to Seek a Life Sentence for a Juvenile

In terms of practical implementation, we propose that the Department create a committee of experienced attorneys to review all requests to seek life sentences for juvenile offenders. This proposal is modeled after the Department's capital case review process. As outlined in the *Justice Manual*, federal decisions to seek the death penalty are reviewed by the Capital Review Committee (CRC), which in turn makes recommendations to the Attorney General through the Deputy Attorney General. *See* U.S. Dep't of Just., Just. Manual §9-10.130 (2021). The CRC comprises attorneys from the Office of the Deputy Attorney General, the Office of the Assistant Attorney General for the Criminal Division, the U.S. Attorneys' Offices, and other components within the Department. *Id.* By centralizing the recommendation process and drawing attorneys from diverse backgrounds, the CRC promotes the just and consistent application of capital sentencing laws, while minimizing the prospects of arbitrariness and reliance on impermissible factors. *See id.* §9-10.030 (describing the purposes of the capital case review process).

We believe that the Department should take a similar approach to juvenile life sentences. As with the death penalty for an adult, a life-without-parole sentence for a juvenile is the ultimate punishment. And life sentences are imposed sufficiently infrequently in the federal system that it would not be unduly burdensome for the Department to conduct an individualized review in each case. Unless a juvenile offender is one of those rare children incapable of rehabilitation, the Department should deny a request to seek a life sentence.

We believe the review process should contain at least the following elements:

- Federal prosecutors should be required to submit a request to the committee before seeking a life sentence for a juvenile offender. That submission should include not only the prosecutor's reasons for seeking the sentence, but also any relevant materials provided by defense counsel.

- All requests should be reviewed by a committee composed similarly to the CRC, but that also includes attorneys with expertise relating to juveniles. The committee should include, for example, members from the Organized Crime and Gang Section of the Criminal Division—which has experience relating to the prosecution of juveniles—and the Special Litigation Section of the Civil Rights Division—which has experience relating to juvenile justice. *See id.* §§8-2.263, 9-8.001.

- The Attorney General should make the final decision as to whether a life sentence should be sought in each case. As with the capital case review process, securing sign-off at the highest level is necessary to ensure adequate consideration before requesting the most severe penalty.

The committee should also conduct regular, proactive reviews of juvenile offenders serving life sentences in the federal system. Although we have not analyzed each of the underlying cases in detail, our preliminary assessment suggests that some of these individuals do not deserve their severe punishments because subsequent events have demonstrated that they have some capacity to change and thus are not among the permanently incorrigible.

To give just one example, Riley Briones, Jr. was a juvenile offender who was sentenced to life before *Miller* and was resentenced to life following *Miller*. His sentence was subsequently vacated by the en banc Ninth Circuit, *see United States v. Briones*, 929 F.3d 1057 (9th Cir. 2019) (en banc), but the Ninth Circuit's decision was in turn vacated by the Supreme Court for further consideration in light of *Jones*, *see United States v. Briones*, 141 S. Ct. 2589 (2021) (mem.). On remand, Mr. Briones compellingly explained not only that he is capable of rehabilitation, but also that he has in fact improved himself in prison. For example, he has received his GED, counseled younger inmates, and maintained a spotless disciplinary record. *See* Appellant's Supplemental Brief at 4, *United States v. Briones*, No. 16-10150 (9th Cir. June 25, 2021). The government conceded that Mr. Briones had improved himself—and thus that he is not irretrievably depraved—but it nevertheless argued that Mr. Briones's life sentence should stand. *See id.* at 5–6. The district court likewise acknowledged that Mr. Briones had changed, but it resentenced him to life in prison. *See id.* at 6. On December 6, 2021, the Ninth Circuit affirmed Mr. Briones's life sentence, *see United States v. Briones*, 18 F.4th 1170 (9th Cir. 2021), and he is currently seeking rehearing en banc.

We urge the Department (whether through our proposed committee or other channels) to reconsider its position in Mr. Briones's case, and to consider advocating for sentence reductions for other juvenile offenders currently serving life sentences. Where an individual's sentence is still being reviewed on direct appeal (as is Mr. Briones's), the Department should seek to return the case to the district court for resentencing, unless the committee concludes that the offender is incapable of rehabilitation. And where an individual's sentence has become final, the Department should explore available mechanisms for correcting that sentence. *See, e.g.*, 18 U.S.C. § 3582(c)(1)(A)(i) (authorizing a district court to reduce a defendant's sentence if it finds that "extraordinary and compelling reasons warrant such a reduction"). The Department should also consider recommending sentence commutations for juvenile offenders capable of rehabilitation whose sentences have become final.

In addition to reviewing the sentences of juvenile offenders formally serving life in prison, we note there are strong arguments for reviewing the sentences of those serving lengthy terms of years. Focusing on a broader group may be necessary to avoid unwarranted disparities that could result if individuals serving formal life sentences are eligible for regular review, while those serving functional life sentences are not. Furthermore, it may be unfair to deprive a juvenile offender of any opportunity for review simply because a prosecutor did not technically seek, and a court did not technically impose, a formal life sentence.

Conclusion

Violent crime warrants proportionate punishment. But justice demands that any such punishment reflect an offender's youth and capacity for rehabilitation. Based on our experience as prosecutors, Department of Justice officials, and judges, we believe that life without parole is appropriate only in rare cases of permanent incorrigibility. Where a juvenile offender is capable of rehabilitation—as nearly all will be—we urge the Department to advocate for a lesser sentence.

Sincerely,

Roy L. Austin, Jr., former Deputy Assistant to the President for the Office of Urban Affairs, Justice, and Opportunity; former Deputy Assistant Attorney General for the Civil Rights Division; former Assistant U.S. Attorney, U.S. Attorney's Office for the District of Columbia

Donald B. Ayer, former Deputy Attorney General of the United States; former U.S. Attorney for the Eastern District of California

William G. Bassler, former Judge, U.S. District Court for the District of New Jersey

Buta Biberaj, Commonwealth's Attorney, Loudoun County, Virginia

Shay Bilchik, former Associate Deputy Attorney General and Administrator, Office of Juvenile Justice and Delinquency Prevention, U.S. Department of Justice; former Chief Assistant State Attorney, 11th Judicial Circuit (Miami-Dade County), Florida

Sherry Boston, District Attorney, Stone Mountain Judicial Circuit (DeKalb County), Georgia

Chesa Boudin, District Attorney, San Francisco, California

Michael R. Bromwich, former Inspector General, U.S. Department of Justice; former Chief, Narcotics Unit, U.S. Attorney's Office for the Southern District of New York

A. Bates Butler III, former U.S. Attorney for the District of Arizona

Bonnie Campbell, former Attorney General, State of Iowa

Real Life Stories

Kami N. Chavis, former Assistant U.S. Attorney, U.S. Attorney's Office for the District of Columbia

John Choi, Ramsey County Attorney, Minnesota

W.J. Michael Cody, former U.S. Attorney for the Western District of Tennessee; former Attorney General, State of Tennessee

James M. Cole, former Deputy Attorney General of the United States

Michael Cotter, former U.S. Attorney for the District of Montana

William B. Cummings, former U.S. Attorney, Eastern District of Virginia

Michael H. Dettmer, former U.S. Attorney for the Western District of Michigan

Thomas J. Donovan, Jr., Attorney General, State of Vermont; former State's Attorney, Chittenden County, Vermont

Michael T. Dougherty, District Attorney, Twentieth Judicial District (Boulder County) Colorado

Peter Edelman, former Special Assistant to the Assistant Attorney General, U.S. Department of Justice; former Director, New York State Division for Youth

George C. Eskin, former Judge, Santa Barbara County Superior Court, California; former Assistant District Attorney, Ventura and Santa Barbara Counties, California; former Chief Assistant City Attorney, Criminal Division, City of Los Angeles, California

John Farmer, former Attorney General, State of New Jersey; former Assistant U.S. Attorney, U.S. Attorney's Office for the District of New Jersey

Noel Fidel, former Chief Judge, Arizona Court of Appeals, Division One; former Presiding Civil Judge, Superior Court of Maricopa County, Arizona

Lisa Foster, former Judge, California Superior Court; former Director, Office for Access to Justice, U.S. Department of Justice

Gil Garcetti, former District Attorney, Los Angeles County, California

Sarah F. George, State's Attorney, Chittenden County, Vermont

Mark Gonzalez, District Attorney, Nueces County, Texas

James P. Gray, former Judge, Superior Court of Orange County, California; former Assistant U.S. Attorney, U.S. Attorney's Office for the Central District of California

Gary G. Grindler, former Acting Deputy Attorney General of the United States; former Deputy Assistant Attorney General for the Criminal Division, Principal Associate Deputy Attorney General, Chief of Staff to the Attorney General, and Deputy Assistant Attorney General for the Civil Division, U.S. Department of Justice; former Assistant U.S. Attorney, U.S. Attorney's Office for the Southern District of New York; former Assistant U.S. Attorney, U.S. Attorney's Office for the Northern District of Georgia

Nancy Guthrie, former Judge, Ninth Judicial District, Wyoming

Andrea Harrington, District Attorney, Berkshire County, Massachusetts

John Hummel, District Attorney, Deschutes County, Oregon

Tim Johnson, former U.S. Attorney for the Southern District of Texas

Neal Katyal, former Acting Solicitor General of the United States

Peter Keisler, former Acting Attorney General of the United States; former Assistant Attorney General for the Civil Division and Acting Associate Attorney General, U.S. Department of Justice

Miriam Aroni Krinsky, former Assistant U.S. Attorney and Chief, Criminal Appeals Section, U.S. Attorney's Office for the Central District of California; former Chair, Solicitor General's Advisory Group on Appellate Issues

Corinna Lain, former Assistant Commonwealth's Attorney, Richmond, Virginia

Scott Lassar, former U.S. Attorney for the Northern District of Illinois

Steven H. Levin, former Assistant U.S. Attorney and Deputy Chief, Criminal Division, U.S. Attorney's Office for the District of Maryland; former Assistant U.S. Attorney, U.S. Attorney's Office for the Middle District of North Carolina

J. Alex Little, former Assistant U.S. Attorney, Middle District of Tennessee; former Assistant U.S. Attorney, District of Columbia

Rory K. Little, former Associate Deputy Attorney General, U.S. Department of Justice; former Assistant U.S. Attorney and Chief, Appellate Section, U.S. Attorney's Office for the Northern District of California; former Trial Attorney, Organized Crime & Racketeering Strike Force, U.S. Department of Justice

Beth McCann, District Attorney, 2nd Judicial District (Denver County), Colorado

Mary B. McCord, former Acting Assistant Attorney General and Principal Deputy Assistant Attorney General for National Security, U.S. Department of Justice; former Assistant U.S. Attorney and Chief, Criminal Division, U.S. Attorney's Office for the District of Columbia

Michael D. McKay, former U.S. Attorney for the Western District of Washington

J. Tom Morgan, former District Attorney, DeKalb County, Georgia

Jerome O'Neill, former Acting U.S. Attorney, District of Vermont; former Assistant U.S. Attorney, U.S. Attorney's Office for the District of Vermont

David W. Ogden, former Deputy Attorney General of the United States; former Assistant Attorney General for the Civil Division, U.S. Department of Justice

Wendy Olson, former U.S. Attorney for the District of Idaho

Stephen M. Orlofsky, former Judge, U.S. District Court for the District of New Jersey

Terry L. Pechota, former U.S. Attorney for the District of South Dakota

Joseph Platania, Commonwealth's Attorney, City of Charlottesville, Virginia

Karl A. Racine, Attorney General for the District of Columbia

Ira Reiner, former District Attorney, Los Angeles County, California; former City Attorney, City of Los Angeles, California

Heidi Rummel, Director, Post-Conviction Justice Project; former Assistant U.S. Attorney, U.S. Attorney's Office for the Central District of California; former Assistant U.S. Attorney, U.S. Attorney's Office for the District of Columbia

Barry Schneider, former Judge, Maricopa County Superior Court, Arizona

Kevin H. Sharp, former Chief Judge, U.S. District Court for the Middle District of Tennessee

Carol A. Siemon, Prosecuting Attorney, Ingham County, Michigan

Shannon Taylor, Commonwealth's Attorney, Henrico County, Virginia

Marsha Ternus, former Chief Justice, Supreme Court of Iowa

Raúl Torrez, District Attorney, Bernalillo County, New Mexico

Joyce White Vance, former U.S. Attorney for the Northern District of Alabama

Atlee W. Wampler III, former U.S. Attorney for the Southern District of Florida; former Attorney-In-Charge, Miami Organized Crime Strike Force, Criminal Division, U.S. Department of Justice

Andrew H. Warren, State Attorney, Thirteenth Judicial Circuit (Tampa), Florida

One of the most destructive patterns in 'correctional' facilities is that they are too often the cause of trauma rather than positive change. Correctional facilities, it may be argued, are not designed for anything other than being places where great fear, trauma, and even abuse is created, encouraged, and sustained under the guise of 'correction'. And, some members of the greater public believe that this is the right way to deal with the incarcerated, negating (through ignorance) the very real circumstances and systems that lead our children directly into prisons in the first place. In other words, taking a high moral stance cannot take away from the very real damage that holding humans in captivity is causing, not only to the one being held, but to their families as well. It is also a travesty that *habeous corpus* is often overlooked.

A destructive system is why it is no surprise that often the kind of people hired to carry out the controlling (and often abusive) measures behind the walls of these institutions (beyond the sights of society) are the very kind of people who have the capacity and desire to inflict humiliation and punishment on others, and even derive pleasure out of it.

The Sheriff at *Bexar County Jail* (detention centre for juveniles) in San Antonio, Texas is one example. In a documentary made by *Java Films*, she boastfully asks youth partaking in a *Shock Program* for high-school teens, *"You ever seen anyone hog-tied before? We do that. If my Lieutenant tells me I'm allowed to hog-tie someone, it's like Christmas!"* And when the tensions inside get to be too much, Lieutenant Spangler lets the teens know that a combat unit (adults dressed like futuristic soldiers) will get deployed, *"You wanna fight somebody, they have no problem using force on you, tasing you, pepper-spraying you, pepper balling you, the chair — one way or another you're gonna do what we want...for two hours you'll be locked up like that [in a hog-tie position] and left in your cell."* The main problem is that prisons are a place that draws (among others) no shortage of people who enjoy subjugating and humiliating other humans.

Numerous transgressions and illegal offences have been illicited by those in power, against those of apparent lesser moral substance, such as beatings, rape, torture, psychological trauma, arbitrary strip searches, and other humiliations, with impunity. The main difference today, in dealing with those who have transgressed social norms and laws (whether guilty or not), versus throughout history is that today the level of control has become very systematized and industrialized. *They know not what they do*, shamefully, has become the norm.

With high-levels of recitivism (re-offence), it may be time to consider whether we should stop denying that punitive measures have never deterred crime (because the cause of crime is not a low moral fibre). In other words, punishing via violence (into high-morality) is impossible because committing punishment is itself a form of violence and, thereby, considered to be immoral.

When it comes to the rights of the child, the US is the only country in the world that has not adopted the United Nations convention on the rights of the child. *See: https://www.ohchr.org/en/instruments-mechanisms/instruments/convention-rights-child.*

Children in the US can be tried, convicted, and housed in the same 'correctional' facilities as adults, where they are at a higher risk of being raped by adults, along with a higher risk for suicide.

"We have to start treating kids like kids and not like inmates. If we talk about kids as inmates, then we're going to treat them like inmates. If we talk about kids as young people here, and giving them an opportunity to change, and then our attitudes will change about how we treat them."

*~ **Susan Burke, Director***
Juvenile Justice Services

The UN also continues to denounce cruel practices in US jails. In New York (where the Statue of Liberty stands), juveniles are routinely forced into solitary confinement. *"The DOC appears to routinely resort to repressive measures, such as prolonged or indefinite isolation, excessive use of in-cell restraints and needlessly intrusive strip searches. There seems to be a State-sanctioned policy aimed at purposefully inflicting severe pain or suffering, physical or mental, which may well amount to torture."*

For more information, see: *https://www.ohchr.org/en/press-releases/2020/02/united-states-prolonged-solitary-confinement-amounts-psychological-torture*

"Although the juvenile court was established in 1899 with the purpose of treating juveniles who commit crimes differently from adults, the division between juvenile and adult courts has eroded significantly over time. Juveniles are now routinely tried in adult court, according to the same rules that apply to adult defendants. If convicted, they face the same sentences as adults, with some narrow exceptions. A quarter [there remains 75%] of the juvenile offenders serving LWOP in the United States received this sentence due to felony murder convictions... The Court's guiding principles in these cases have been informed by an emerging body of research that establishes that "fundamental differences between juvenile and adult minds" diminish the culpability of juvenile offenders... Based on adolescent brain development research, the Supreme Court has determined that juveniles', *"irresponsible conduct is not as morally reprehensive as that of an adult."*

~ **Caldwell, B., Law Professor**
The Twice Diminished Culpability of Juvenile Accomplices to Felony Murder. UC Irvine Law Review, 11(4), 905 (2021)

Dialogue Prompts:

1. What is the purpose of prisons? Do people retain their natural rights as humans? What are natural rights vs governed rights?

2. Is criminality a problem of low morality? What is morality?

3. What are the underlying complications that lead to transgressions?

4. Should females who are pregnant be incarcerated? And, is it fair to the well-being of the unborn baby, and their natural rights? What are a baby's govered rights as they pertain to being born incarcerated?

5. Is it accurate to reference youth in the criminal justice system as 'troubled delinquents'? Is that a misattribution? And does that distract from the very real consideration that society itself is troubled? How do the conditions youth are in (family, school, work, social) impact their actions?

6. Is it possible, and if so, how do we look at human behaviour as beyond the domain of psychology or psychiatry? Is it, for instance, every adult's personal responsibility to prioritize understanding of human nature as a fundamental groundwork for a healthy and functioning community, and society?

"People don't realize what's really going on in this country. There are a lot of things that are going on that are unjust. People aren't being held accountable. And that's something that needs to change. That's something that this country stands for: freedom, liberty and justice for all."

~ *Colin R. Kaepernick*
American Civil Rights Activist & Football Quarterback

"Injustice anywhere is a threat to justice everywhere."

~ *Martin Luther King Jr. (1929-1968)*
American Baptist Minister & Humanist

"There is always light, if only we're brave enough to see it. If only we are brave enough to be it."

~ *Amanda Gorman*
American Poet & Activist

"Some find pleasure in the infliction of torture; others, like Buddha, feel that they cannot be completely happy so long as any living thing is suffering. Most people divide mankind emotionally into friends and enemies, feeling sympathy for the former, but not for the latter. An ethic such as that of Christianity or Buddhism has its emotional basis in universal sympathy."

~ Bertrand A.W. Russell (1872-1970)
Philosopher & Mathematician

4

Possibilities
Directions & Actions

If we take seriously into consideration that we live in a society that has been constructed under the framework of a violent patriarchy, where punishment is central, then we may also take into consideration that the social system can be balanced into a healthy construction — one which is based in logic and rationale rather than fear and dissociation. The irrationality, for instance, of mis-spending billions in resources that could be used to prevent harm from happening in the first place, must take precedence.

For instance, the national average cost to incarcerate a young person in the US is $215,000; in Canada, $120,000; and in the UK between £140,000-300,000; and these figures vary slightly for adult males and females.

It is clear from the numbers, and social and economic standpoints, that incarceration is simply disastrous (*along with keeping people in poverty, which is another form of incarceration: e.g. homelessness, which contributes to transgressions, often due to social or economic emergencies*). And, we can very easily see that it does not make rational sense to mis-apply precious resources to construct violent inner societies within the walls of the prisons in the name of punishment — this happens as a direct consequence of the entire manner in which the system is devised: it is a *dysfuctional* system. Moreover, the exercise of incarceration itself further exacerbates harm to society by not properly appreciating that habituating inmates to a kind of life that no human ought to live, often infringing on their human rights, and then releasing them into the mainstream because 'time has been served', is itself irresponsible and reckless. Do you believe lawmakers are accountable?

Members of the public must consider that no matter how greatly society may want retribution for crimes committed, there is no rational, social, or economic justification for creating a worse situation on the inside by investing in the *prison industrial complex* where retributive harm is being justified. This formula does not solve any problems. Instead, it exacerbates them, and then regurgitates them back onto society. And, it is also primitive in its level of sophistication, where the cycle of violence continues in perpetuity.

Going forward, let's consider that top-down measures for handling the incarcerated actually begins with the formation of communities and families. And, that what we see in those who commit crimes or even misdemeanours is a consequence of top-down societal arrangement and control. We can no longer believe that a 'moral-brokenness' in those locked-up is the real reason for their transgressions. We must all look at the moral-brokenness of those in power, who design and sustain the very systems that people with less power have to live under, and the eventual consequences that affect us all.

Consciousness in integrity and rationale is the basis of a sane society.

What is required, in order to move from a place of complacency to action then is motivation — both inspired from the inside and outside of one's self. We often do not realize that we are in a kind of prison in our own mind, where we do not know who we really are and our true power as a human being. Fyodor Dostoevsky is famously quoted, *"The best way to keep a prisoner from escaping is to make sure he never knows he's in prison."* That is the spell of systemic patriarchy over men, women, and children alike. The inculcation is that we are normal and healthy as we are, and to never trust our natural instincts (*intuition*) that informs us otherwise. Community-less urban settings condition us into believing our lives are worth nothing more than to feed an insatiable desire for contentment in things that will never be met. And, distraction from our human essence is the vice that is used.

Instead, I argue, that we are are great love and wonder itself. And, that we are so mind-occupied that, in this way, we are distracted from our true nature. We are actually designed to explore the world, not rule over it; to

"Retributive theory believes that pain will vindicate, but in practice that is often counterproductive for both victim and offender. Restorative justice theory, on the other hand, argues that what truly vindicates is acknowledgment of victims' harms and needs, combined with an active effort to encourage offenders to take responsibility, make right the wrongs, and address the causes of their behavior. By addressing this need for vindication in a positive way, restorative justice has the potential to affirm both victim and offender and to help them transform their lives."

~ Howard Zehr, Author
The Little Book of Restorative Justice

interact with others, not try to control them; and to create beauty not war. To unlock the cell we are living in — whether of our own making, or someone else's — a commitment to honouring our true nature is the key.

The Spirit Level (2010) is a book about equality, community, and humanity. In it, the following passage:

> The idea that we can't have both liberty and equality seems to have emerged during the Cold War. What the state-owned economics of Eastern Europe and the Soviet Union seemed to show was that greater equality could only be gained at the expense of freedom. An important ideological cost of the Cold War was that America gave up its historical commitment to equality. For the first Americans, as for Thomas Paine [1737-1839], you couldn't have true liberty without equality. Without one you could not have the other. Slavery, as the simultaneous denial of both, proved that rule. Equality was the bastion against arbitrary power. The scale of economic inequality which exists today is less an expression of freedom and democracy as of their denial. The truth is that modern inequality exists because democracy is excluded from the economic sphere.

For more information, see: https://equalitytrust.org.uk

In the 19th Century, Karl Marx (1818-1883), put forward his *Theory of Alienation*, which referred to a human's alienation from their true essence as a result of being reduced to a mechanistic cog in a social-class-hierarchy. This alienation can be thought of as a kind of indebtedness to a social system rather than developing one's self as an autonomous being who is self-directed. If, in other words, people are enslaved into a system that will not afford them the freedom from ever-seeking food, shelter, and safety, then they cannot actualize themselves and, as a result, become alienated from their essence. In other words, people are well more than cheap labourers for the 'upper-class', and have a depth that needs to be realized: the direction of one life by another — 'control over' — is not natural, it is against nature.

What we are seeing in the current breakdown of society, is a further and further control over people. A breakdown of our inner-nature.

Marx listed four kinds of alienation (separation), which Gabor Mate (Humanist and Author) explained, in contex, during his 2012 talk at *Bioneers*, see: *https://bioneers.org/dr-gabor-mate-toxic-culture-bioneers/*

1. **Alienation from nature.** Our consumer and economic-growth system are based on the extraction of the natural resources, and it further alienates us from nature.

2. **Alienation from other people.** As years go by, people have less contact, less intimacy, less trust, less of a sense of relationship. And that leads to increased capacity for illness (physical and mental).

3. **Alienation from our work.** A lot of people no longer do work that has any meaning to them. Since human beings are productive creatures — we really are created in the image of God, we are meant to create — when we do work that is not creative and does not reflect who we are, that imposes depression, anxiety, sense of meaninglessness. And when we have a sense of meaninglessness, we want to substitute that meaning that we have lost by all kinds of other activities. And then people get hung up on how they look, how other people feel about them, what they possess, what successes they will achieve, in other words, all the false substitutes, which cannot possibly compensate for the lack of genuine meaning. And, much of the economy is designed to sell us things to substitute for this lack of meaning.

4. **Alienation from ourselves.** At some point during our childhood, we get disconnected from our instincts [*intuition*]. That means that in this culture, something very powerful happens to alienate you from your true self. Because the world couldn't stand who you really were. And your parents were too stressed themselves to honour and recognize who you really were. Then we become alienated from ourselves, we shut down our gut feelings — and our gut feelings are not luxuries — they tell us what is right and what is wrong, they tell us what is dangerous and what is safe, and they tell us what is true and what is false. So, when we are alienated from our gut feelings we no longer have a sense of reality or a sense of truth.

Mate emphasized that the above alienations are a by-product when society is set up to sell a lot of products that substitute for a loss of meaning and that, in fact, much of our economy is based on and feeds off our loss of meaning in ourselves, and in our communities, and our cultures.

"To be a human being among people, and to remain one forever, no matter in what circumstances, not to grow despondent and not to lose heart — that's what life is all about, that's its task."

~ *Fyodor Dostoevsky (1821-1881)*
 Russian Novelist & Humanist

"Those people who see clearly the necessity of changed thinking must themselves undertake the discipline of thinking in new ways and must persuade others to do so."

~ *Kathleen Lonsdale (1903-1971)*
Physicist & Prison Reformer

Maya Schenwar

Source: TEDxBaltimore, 2016

The following is an excerpt from a talk given by Maya Schenwar, a Journalist and Writer (Truthout.org), whose work in the area of carceral abolition gets us to think about incarceration by pointing out some key factors for consideration:

> Imagine a country in which millions of people live inside cages. These cages are located far from their homes and families, often in the middle of remote corn fields. Some people are caged for 5 years, 10 years, 20 years, sometimes their entire lives. It's not just anyone that ends up in a cage, it's the society's most marginalized people — people who are already oppressed, already vulnerable. I'm not actually taking about an imaginary country, I'm referring to the United States of America. This country contains less than 5% of the world's population, yet almost 25% of the global prison population. And, 10 million children in this country, have experienced parental incarceration — they have been torn from a parent. Beyond that, 70 thousand children have themselves been living in cages. Prison is not 'correctional', prison is a cycle.

Schenwar explains that the cycle of prison functions in four main ways:

1. **That policing is the gateway to prison that ensures a steady supply of people flowing into prisons;**

2. **That many of the people who commit the acts society refers to as 'crimes' are doing so in the service of their own survival.**

> Prison does nothing to address poverty, or economic injustice. Actually, people coming out of prison have even fewer resources, and even fewer opportunities than they did going in. Plus, they are emerging from prison with a "felon" label, and that label makes them even less able to get jobs, housing,

and education. And, very often, they return to criminalized acts in order to survive.

3. **That hurt people hurt people.** When we think about the people who are incarcerated for violent crimes, often we don't think about the fact that most of them have been victims of violence in the past. Prison does not help people heal. Actually, prison continues the violence that people have experienced. I am talking about the various acts of physical and sexual violence that take place behind bars — many of them actually perpetrated by authorities. But, also we need to keep in mind that caging a human being is in itself a violent act. The trauma of prison stays with people after prison, and perpetuates that cycle of harm and violence.

4. **That prison cuts off connections, it isolates people from the world.** When you cut someone off from their family, and their loved ones, and their community, you are setting them up for failure. You are cutting the ties that provide support and motivation. Even the *Bureau of Prisons* recognizes this. They say that the number one predictor of whether or not someone will re-offend, is whether they have support from their family. But, what they don't acknowledge is that prison itself breaks down those vital links.

Schenwar points out that the children of incarcerated parents are more likely to live in poverty, drop out of school, and to go to prison themselves. And that, "*Prison produces more prison. We can see this in the fact that the correctional system has not corrected itself out of existence. Instead, it has grown — it has expanded by 500% over the past forty years. Mainstream Social Scientists are saying that prison is criminogenic — it causes crime.*"

> We need to think about victims of crime for crimes in which there is a victim. Prison might provide some sense of vindication and temporary safety — we do need practices of accountability in our society. But, prison does not provide reparations for the harm, resources for them to heal, or even an apology. And since prison is a place that promotes harm and violence, it certainly does not provide victims with any indication that the harm will not happen again.

◆

Jennifer Thomas

Source: TEDxNorthCentralCollege, 2017

"I discovered my passion for prison reform when I spent four months in *Winnebago County Jail* awaiting a bond reduction hearing. In August 2011, I was arrested in connection with the overdose death of my best friend. I was a passenger in his vehicle when he purchased the heroin that would later kill him. In jail, I became intimately acquainted with the criminal justice system, jail culture, and the plight of the prisoner. That experience profoundly changed the direction of my life. Upon release, I made it my life's mission to use my experiences to help others, specifically prisoners and addicts."

In this illuminating talk, Thomas shared the many injustices she witnessed in only four months while awaiting processing in the carceral system in the United States of America. She shares being locked down for serveral days due to under-staffing; that dental issues were handled by pulling out teeth;

and witnessing the denial of due process because *Public Defenders* do not have enough time to handle their case.

Thomas then compared the US system to the Norweigan system after having toured their system as part of field research regarding incarceration, and was pleasantly made aware of key differences. The maximum security compound itself is made as much like living areas in non-carceral settings as possible, with no bars on the doors, each unit having its own kitchen, and each 'cell' designed as a simple dorm room, with a private bathroom.

Notably, Thomas reported two other notable differences: 1.) that the civil rights of each incarcerated person is held, *e.g. education, healthcare, and voting*; and 2.) that the role of the prison guard was that of *Contact Officer*, who was assigned to a few people at a time in order to communicate with them on an individual level.

The model for *prevention through communication* is also a key difference between the US and Norweigan models that Thomas pointed out. The idea behind this model is based on research that human-to-human understanding and communication reduces stress, anxiety, and dissociative behaviour.

Thomas said of the US penal system:

"As long as we continue our punitive approach to prison, we will continue to churn out toxicity, it is just as simple as that. It is time for a change. It is time for us to come to our senses."

Jeff Wallace

Source: TEDxNaperville, 2016

Wallace provides a chilling and redemptive account of his life through the juvenile criminal system, from his first time being incarcerated alongside adults, the consequences, and his insights, to the work he is commited and inspired to continue with today.

"It all started when the metal door slammed shut onto the cell. It sent shivers down my spine. The chamber was cold and it smelled of stale air. You know, there's something about a door slamming shut that provides an eerie level of finality and reflection. You hear the echo of it in your mind for a long time to come. And, as that door slammed, I started remembering all that advice that my parents and my teachers gave me, and I ignored it. And there I was, with plenty of time to reflect on all that information that I had met with disbelief, laughter, and scorn."

Wallace shares, in detail, the offence for which he was convicted as a youth of 17 years — a combination of robbery and assault. He was tried and convicted as an adult, and sentenced to eleven years.

"I watched grown men melt into puddles of insanity as their minds could no longer take the conditions of the monotony of being in solitary confinement. I watched massive amounts of violence that included guards beating prisoners, prisoners being stabbed, and all this before I turned 18."

While in solitary confinement, he recalls playing chess and contemplating on four virtues of life:

1. *respect everybody*: no matter what their differences; respect each individual piece (using a chessboard as analogy); and understand that each square a person is in is an important square.

2. *protect the weak:* you may look at the pawn, and it may appear at the beginning of the game as the weakest piece, but it actually has the most potential, more than any other piece on the board to actually become the most powerful piece.

3. **be humble:** play the game as if every move counts, and that's how you make decisions in life — don't take it as a given.

4. **practice restraint:** when playing the game, do not chase pieces; play the game to win.

Wallace came to the conclusion after many communications, through a vent, with a fellow inmate in solitary confinement that his redemption would be gained through education, perseverance, and being in the service of others.

Of the greatest insights Wallace shares is about the need to understand how trauma affects humans in dynamic ways. *"We have to then introduce trauma-informed care. If you take anything from what I've said, I want you to take this; when you look at these kids, when you look at them, even the adults, these young adults, I want you to look at them, and instead of saying, "What's wrong with you?" I want you to ask, "What happened to you?"*

Wallace emphasizes the need to understand brain development of youth, and the effects of trauma on the brain. Many of the youth have experienced multiple forms of violence and trauma, which affects the senses, interpretations, and behaviour.

Another of the many important messages Wallace shares is juvenile interaction in adult settings: *"This is one of the more personal things for me, is that we cannot allow juveniles to be with adults in prison settings. I have to tell you that when I first went to the Iowa State Penitentiary... I was still 17, the neighbor to my right, his name was "Shank", he's doing a life sentence. Neighbor to my left, he's doing a life sentence, and he just shanked somebody. So what we've got then is, this is who is influencing our kids when we put them in there. Then, my first cellmate was a 50-year old man, who was in there for second-degree murder — and I'm 17. Again, he had the whole thing going on, from the "three-time loser" on his arms, to, you know, everything going on. That was my roommate; that was my cellmate. We cannot continue to house juveniles and adults together. That's wrong."*

Wallace formally earned his bachelor and master degrees in Criminal Justice since being released. He now oversees, as Group Care Manager, a team of over 50 employees working with juveniles *"that include case-workers, program supervisors, residential counselors, and nighttime workers."* His work includes advocating for a trauma-informed approach, strengthening individuals, families, and communities at large through creative and effective methods. Additionally, Wallace also works as a Youth Counselor at a County Detention Center in Iowa, and as Crisis Interventionist for the Davenport Police Department and local hospitals.

Wallace concluded on the importance of building community:

"We need to re-establish community connections. Those community connections have to involve job opportunities, they have to involve the ability to complete education, because school was one of my saviors. And they also have to be able to engage in community service. Everybody here has a choice, and that choice is simple. You can either continue to invest in prisons, and we do, a lot, don't we? We invest in a lot of prisons. Or we can invest in our children."

Community

Community has changed drastically in just the past century. This has affected how we rely on one another, our level of interaction, and certainly the depth of our connections; and, has even dysregulated our physiologies. What impact do you think this may be having on the emotional experiences, expectations, behaviours, and even levels of ailments, due to the social construct of living in the 'modern' world? How might these impacts be mitigated? And, how can we reduce *othering*, while increasing connections in genuine ways?

Self-taught historian and proprietor, Jonathan Townsend, had this to say about the differences in community in history as compared with today:

> Do you have what it takes to live in a small community? To be part of that community? To actually do something that the community needs. A lot of times we are thinking about what we can get at the local store — 'I need something, where can I get it?' Rarely do we think the opposite direction, which is, '*What do my neighbours need, and can I supply that to them?*' So, that's part of living in a small community. In the 21st century today, we do not live in small communities. End of story. We may have a 'community' around us, people around us, but we don't need them to survive.
>
> *That's part of what a community is — people that rely upon one another.*
>
> So, I don't rely on local community, my neighbours. No one of my neighbours gives me any of the things I need for survival: water, food, clothing, shelter — those things don't necessarily come from my neighbour. Most people probably shop at some kind of big box store, and the food that is in a large grocery store, that's coming from all over the United States — most of it's probably grown more than 500 miles away from where I'm at...very little of it is coming from, you know, 10 miles away. And, if I go to a store to buy clothing, well certainly none of the clothing that's in any of my local stores is made in the United States — the cloth

isn't, and the items themselves are not sewn here. Shoes? No, nobody is locally making shoes where I live. And, for shelter, certainly there are plenty of contractors and plumbers and what not, but none of the materials they use are locally sourced. I don't think very much lumber comes from right around here, at least for normal building trades; and, nails, or screws, or tools — nope, they come from all over the world. Who knows where the tools come from, or the individual components that we use for constructing a house.

That's not true in the 18th Century. Everyone was living within some kind of small community — even if they were living in the city, or far out on the frontier — there were still these people around them that they needed for their very survival... people that are helping them with food, local farmers, grains, livestock, people that fix things, so black-smiths, people that are weaving and sewing. There's just so much, and of course every, every small town, every small community had someone who, yes, made shoes.

For more information, see: *https://www.youtube.com/watch?v=QJHQmCJMtZY&list=RDC-MUCxr2d4As312LulcajAkKJYw&index=12*

"Mental health is not about the individual, it's about the social context. 50% of adults in this society [US], which considers itself the most successful society in the history of the world, actually suffer from chronic illness; 50% of adolescents are now said to meet the diagnostic criteria for one or another mental health condition, with .5 million on anti-psy-chotic medications; 3.5 million children are receiving stimulant medications for ADHD; in Canada, the number of prescriptions for ADHD has gone up 43% in the past five years."

~ *Gabor Mate*
Humanist & Author

(2012) *source Bioneers: https://www.youtube.com/watch?v=erZhTPkOLb0*

Observations of a Special Education Teacher

I worked in Special Education for almost forty years.

The population I worked with were students with severe emotional challenges, and some on the high functioning end of the autistic spectrum. We tried to keep students from being incarcerated. And, we also worked with students who were incarcerated in some cases; and in those cases, also worked with their parole officers.

The goal of our multidisciplinary team was to reintegrate students who were returning from restrictive settings such as hospitals and residential programs back into the mainstream. We also worked with students who were in danger from being removed from their homes, to stay with their families. To help our students, we had to teach them socially appropriate ways to get their needs met, as well as provide them with an educational remediation program.

Central to our core understanding of our students' situation and how to help them, was Maslow's Hierarchy of Needs.

Those needs are physiological needs, safety needs, love and belonging needs, esteem needs, and self-actualization needs. Due to the extreme challenges our students faced, we dealt a great deal with safety needs.

We made sure that they were adequately fed, and felt safe at home, and at school.

"He who opens a school door, closes a prison."

~ *Victor Hugo (1802-1885)*
Writer & Humanist

What I learned during my career is how important those love and belonging needs are to us all. An essential part of providing that experience for our students was to help them feel heard and valued. This point was proven repeatedly when we had to deal with a violent outburst. Although a seemingly impulsive act, with no or very little thought, we learned to ask a very important question.

That question was, "What was the communicative intent of that act?"

What we found was that the student had experienced some sort of trauma, such as not being fed, being physically attacked, or seeing a physical attack. Once we identified the source of the trauma, and the student felt heard, the violence decreased precipitously. Then we could talk to the student, and teach them how to effectively meet their needs by talking.

This experience taught me that as essential as food, shelter, and clothing are to us, just as important is the need to be heard. I believe it is the first step to healing our students, and applied more broadly, the world.

William Filler, MS
Retired Special Education Teacher

Dialogue Prompts:

1. What does community mean to you? What are the different parts, and their impact? Take some time to write about it.

2. If you were to design society in terms of how we *handle* complexities, what considerations would you need to reflect upon? Consider the flow of streamlined services *versus* structured systems that contain many parts and obstacles — what is the impact in how do they differ? How would the foundations of family, community, education, and work be prioritized? What are the foundations? And, how would you include those who are the most vulnerable in terms of limited physical, emotional, or mental capacity?

3. A government's role is to take care of citizens, and not for citizens to be left to fend for themselves (*otherwise there is no purpose to government*). As such, should everyone be ensured a *secure, safe*, and *stable* home of their own — if so, why? How would this impact an individual, their sense of belonging, their mental, emotional, and physical health, and the overall community? What would the greater benefit to society be if this fundamental security were set into place? Is it worth demanding of administrative governments secure, stable, and safe homes for everyone? How would these changes affect incarceration rates, and the overall health of society?

4. What impact does community have on prevention of transgressions, whether from 'criminals' or 'non-criminals'? And, how does our *mind* play a part in creating a healthy community? What role do *emotions* have? What role does the *ego* play? How do we *nurturingly* include all members of society?

5. Do 'white-collar' crimes differ from 'blue-collar' crimes? How so? For example, if a medical professional commits assault, does it make sense to handle the matter via *malpractice* or the *criminal justice system*? What are the differences in terms of the public's perceptions and their access to justice? Is it fair and just that complaints and reprimands in the medical system are not publicly accessible?

"Abolition is not simply de-carceration, put everybody out onto the street. It is reorganizing how we live our lives together in the world."

~ *Ruth W. Gilmore*
Prison Abolitionist & Scholar

Possibilities

"Regenerative agriculture is not only about regenerating soils. It is about healing relationships, healing history, healing the people who still languish in the shadows of the legacies of colonization."

~ Lyla June
Historical Ecologist, Musician, & Humanist

"We may not be responsible for the world that created our minds, but we can take responsibility for the mind with which we create our world."

~ Gabor Mate
Humanist & Author

"We cannot solve our problems with the same thinking we used when we created them."

*~ **Albert Einstein** (1879-1955)*
Physicist & Humanist

"The quasi-neurotic behavior of the masses, which is an appropriate reaction to current and real, though harmful and unsuitable, living conditions, cannot then be 'cured' by 'analyzing' them. Instead, it demands the transformation and elimination of those very living conditions."

*~ **Erich Fromm** (1900-1980)*
Humanist Philosopher & Psychologist

Colophon

Pixabay Illustrations by: Bianca Van Dijk, Anna Lysenko, Dung Tran, Surut Wattanamaetee, Piyapong Saydaung, RosZie, and TianaZX

p. iv, A Prisoner, by William Dyce, London 1846; British Library Archives

p. 2-3, Pentonville Prisoners Exercising, London 1862

p. 6-7, Chain-gang prisoners, artist unknown

p. 11, Prison Tour, Walkes, UK (1781); Thomas Pennant (1726-1798)

p. 14, Pentonville Prison, London, UK (1895)

p. 24-25, St. John the Baptist in Prison: https://www.artic.edu/artworks/16162/saint-john-the-baptist-in-prison-visited-by-two-disciples
Giovanni di Paolo (1455-1460) / Art Institute Chicago

p. 30-31, The Death of Socrates, in prison, by Charles Alphonse Dusfrenoy, circa 1650, oil on canvas, Uffizi Collection, Florence, Italy. Available online: https://www.wikigallery.org/wiki/painting_216821/Charles-Alphonse-Dufresnoy/The-Death-of-Socrates

p. 44, https://www.alamy.com/paul-gavarni-french-1804-1866-debtors-prison-1840-lithograph-printed-in-black-ink-on-wove-paper-image-8-12-7-78-inches-216-20-cm-image328728349.html?imageid=8CD49854-A1E2-4FB7-AB97-7BFCD6A24E59&p=546931&pn=1&searchId=e62739a4753ef0d45d9e3fa5f9627a98&searchtype=0

p. 49, Billie G. McCune
https://www.phaidon.com/agenda/photography/articles/2015/august/25/billy-mccune-danny-lyons-most-tragic-subject/

References & Resources

Section 1
History & Definitions

Ayers, E. L. (1984). Vengeance and Justice: Crime and Punishment in the 19th-Century American South. New York: Oxford University Press.

Beattie, J. (2001). Policing and Punishment in London, 1660{1750: Urban Crime and the Limits of Terror. Oxford: Oxford University Press.

Berger, D. (2014). Captive Nation: Black Prison Organizing in the Civil Rights Era. University of North Carolina Press.

Bradford, W. (1793). An Inquiry How Far the Punishment of Death Is Necessary in Pennsylvania, With Notes and Illustrations. Philadelphia: T: Dobson.

Bright, C. (1996). The Powers that Punish: Prison and Politics in the Era of the \Big House," 1920-1955. Ann Arbor: University of Michigan Press. Campbell, M. C. and Schoenfeld, H. (2013). The transformation of America's penal order: A historicized political sociology of punishment. American Journal of Sociology, 118(5):1375{1423.

Clemmer, D. (1940). The Prison Community. New York: Holt, Rinehart and Winston.

Cohen, S. (1985). Visions of Social Control: Crime, Punishment and Classification Cambridge: Polity.

Cummins, E. (1994). The Rise and Fall of California's Radical Prison Movement. Stanford, CA: Stanford University Press.

Doll, E. E. (1957). Trial and error at Allegheny: The Western State Penitentiary, 1818-1838 The Pennsylvania Magazine of History and Biography, 81(1):3{27.

Eason, J. M. (2017). Big House on the Prairie: Rise of the Rural Ghetto and Prison Proliferation. Chicago: University of Chicago Press.

Feeley, M. and Rubin, E. (2000). Judicial Policy Making and the Modern State: How the Courts Reformed America's Prisons. Cambridge, MA: Cambridge University Press.

Go man, I. (1961). Asylums. Garden City, NY: Anchor Press.

Goodman, P., Page, J., and Phelps, M. (2017). Breaking the Pendulum: The Long Struggle Over Criminal Justice. New York: Oxford University Press.

Haley, S. (2016). No Mercy Here. The University of North Carolina Press. https://doi.org/10.5149/9781469627601_haley

Hirsch, A. J. (1982). From pillory to penitentiary: The rise of criminal incarceration in early Massachusetts. Michigan Law Review, 80(6):1179{1269.

Hirsch, A. J. (1992). The Rise of the Penitentiary: Prisons and Punishment in Early America. New Haven: Yale University Press.

Irwin, J. (1980). Prisons in Turmoil. Boston: Little, Brown.

Jacobs, J. B. (1977). Stateville: The Penitentiary in Mass Society. Chicago: University of Chicago Press.

Langbein, J. (1976). The historical origins of the sanction of imprisonment for serious crime. The Journal of Legal Studies, 5(1):35{60.

Lewis, O. F. (1922). The Development of American Prisons and Prison Customs, 1776{1845: With Special Reference to Early Institutions in the State of New York. Albany: Prison Association of New York.

Lewis, W. D. (1965). From Newgate to Dannemora: The Rise of the Penitentiary in New York, 1796{1848. Ithaca: Cornell University Press.

LeFlouria, T. L. (2015). Chained in Silence. The University of North Carolina Press. https://doi.org/10.5149/9781469622484_leflouria

Lichtenstein, A. (1996). Twice the Work of Free Labor: The Political Economy of Convict Labor in the New South. London: Verso.

Lynch, M. (2010). Sunbelt Justice: Arizona and the Transformation of American Punishment. Stanford, CA: Stanford University Press.

McGinnis, J. D. (1989). Too Few to Count. Canadian Women in Conflict with the Law. Edited by Ellen Adelberg and Claudia Currie. Vancouver: Press Gang Publishers, 1987. Canadian Journal of Law and Society, 4, 212–214. https://doi.org/10.1017/S0829320100001654

McLennan, R. M. (2008). The Crisis of Imprisonment: Protest, Politics, and the Making of the American Penal State, 1776{1941. New York: Cambridge University Press.

Melossi, D. and Pavarini, M. (1981). The Prison and the Factory: Origins of the Penitentiary System. Totowa, NJ: Barnes and Noble Books.

Meranze, M. (1996). Laboratories of Virtue: Punishment, Revolution, and Authority in Philadelphia, 1760{1835. Chapel Hill: University of North Carolina Press.

Oshinsky, D. (1997). Worse Than Slavery: Parchman Farm and the Ordeal of Jim Crow Justice. New York: Free Press.

Pennsylvania (1776). Constitution of Pennsylvania - September 28, 1776. Avalon Project at Yale Law School, Lillian Goldman Law Library. http://avalon.law.yale.edu/18th_century pa08.asp

Pisciotta, A. (1994). Benevolent Repression: Social Control and the American Reformatory-Prison Movement. New York: New York University Press.

Polizzi, D. (2017). The Development History of Solitary and Supermax Confinement. In Solitary confinement (1st ed., p. 31). Policy Press.

Powers, G. (1826). A Brief Account of the Constitution, Management, & Discipline &c. &c. of the New-York State Prison at Auburn. Auburn, NY: U.F. Doubleday.

Rafter, N. (1985). Partial Justice: Women in State Prisons, 1800{1935. Boston: Northeastern University Press.

Rafter, N. H. (1997). Creating Born Criminals. Chicago: University of Illinois Press.

Reiter, K. (2016). 23/7: Pelican Bay Prison and the Rise of Long-Term Solitary Confinement. New Haven: Yale University Press.

Reiter, K. A. (2012). The Most Restrictive Alternative: A Litigation History of Solitary Confinement in U.S. Prisons, 1960–2006. Studies in Law, Politics, and Society, 57, 71–124. https://doi.org/10.1108/S1059-4337(2012)0000057006

Rothman, D. J. (1980). Conscience and Convenience: The Asylum and Its Alternatives in Progressive America. Hawthorne, NY: Aldine de Gruyter.

Rothman, D. J. (2002 [1971]). The Discovery of the Asylum: Social Order and Disorder in the New Republic. New York: Aldine Transaction.

Rubin, A. T. (2018). History of the Prison. In The Handbook of Social Control (pp. 277–292). John Wiley & Sons, Ltd. https://doi.org/10.1002/9781119372394.ch20

Rubin, A. T. (2014). Three waves of American prison development, 1790{1920. In Punishment and Incarceration: A Global Perspective, pages 139{158. Emerald Group Publishing Limited.

Rubin, A. T. (2015). A neo-institutional account of prison di usion. Law & Society Review, 49(2):365{399.

Rubin, A. T. (2018). The prehistory of innovation: A longer view of penal change. Punishment & Society, 20(2):192{216.

Rubin, A. T. (2019). Punishment's legal templates: A theory of formal penal change. Law & Society Review, 53(2):518{553.

Rubin, A. T. (2020). The Deviant Prison: Philadelphia's Eastern State Penitentiary and the Origins of America's Modern Penal System, 1829{1913. Cambridge University Press.

Rubin, A. T. (ND). Innovation and di usion: Theorizing penal change before and after the ideal type. Manuscript in Progress.

Rusche, G. and Kirchheimer, O. (1939 [1968]). Punishment and Social Structure. New York: Columbia University Press.

Schoenfeld, H. (2010). Mass incarceration and the paradox of prison conditions litigation. Law & Society Review, 44(3-4):731{768.

Simon, J. (1993). Poor Discipline: Parole and the Social Control of the Urban Underclass, 1890{1990. Chicago, IL: University of Chicago Press.

Simon, J. (2007). Governing Through Crime: How the War on Crime Transformed American Democracy and Created a Culture of Fear. New York: Oxford University Press.

Spierenburg, P. (1987). From Amsterdam to Auburn: An explanation for the
rise of the prison in seventeenth-century Holland and nineteenth-century America. Journal of Social History, 20(3):439{461.

Spierenburg, P. (1991). The Prison Experience: Disciplinary Institutions and Their Inmates in Early Modern Europe. New Brunswick, NJ: Rutgers.

Sykes, G. M. (2007 [1958]). The Society of Captives: A Study of a Maximum Security.

Tencer, Daniel (July 13, 2012). "Prison Privatization: Canada Mulls Contracting Services To Companies Lobbying For Correctional Work". The Huffington Post Canada.

Todd, W. (2005). "Convict Lease System" Archived September 27, 2008, at the Wayback Machine. In The New Georgia Encyclopedia. Retrieved October 1, 2006.

Zito, M. (December 8, 2003). "Prison Privatization: Past and Present". International Foundation for Protection Officers. Archived from the original on September 23, 2006. Retrieved November 7, 2019.

"Capitalizing on Mass Incarceration: U.S. Growth in Private Prisons". The Sentencing Project.

"Ontario to Take Back Control of Private Super Jail". CBC News. November 10, 2006.

Office of the High Commissioner for Human Rights: https//www.ohcr.org/en/instruments-mechanisms/instruments/basic-principles-treament-prisoners

ACLU: https://www.aclu.org/sites/default/files/field_document/2022-06-15-captivelaborresearchreport.pdf

Females in Prison in the 19th Century: https://brewminate.com/the-treatment-of-women-in-prison-in-the-19th-century/

History of Youth Incarceration:

Britain, Institute of Historical Research: https://archives.history.ac.uk/history-in-focus/welfare/articles/bradleyk.html

Canada, Osgoode Hall Law Journal, York University: https://digitalcommons.osgoode.yorku.ca/cgi/viewcontent.cgi?referer=&httpsredir=1&article=2141&context=ohlj

USA, Centre on Juvenile and Criminal Justice: http://www.cjcj.org/education1/juvenile-justice-history.html

Section 2
Philosophy & Dialogue

Alexander, F., & Staub, H., (1929). Der Verbrecher und sein Richter. Ein psychoanalytischer Einblick in die Welt der Paragraphen, in: T. Moser (Ed.), Psychoanalyse und Justiz, Frankfurt a. M. (Suhrkamp) 1974, pp. 225–433.

Anderson, K., (2000). Erich Fromm and the Frankfort School Critique of Criminal Justice, in K. Anderson & R. Quinney (Eds.), Erich Fromm and the Critical Criminology. Beyond the Punitive Society, Urbana (University of Illinois Press), pp. 83–119.

Bernfeld, S., (1925). Sisyphos oder die Grenzen der Erziehung, Frankfurt a. M. (Suhrkamp) 2012.

Bernfeld, S., (1931). Die Tantalussituation. Bemerkungen zum kriminellen Über-Ich, in: Imago, Vol. 17 (No. 2), pp. 252–267.

Bude, H., (2015). Die Koalition der Angst, in: Frankfurter Allgemeine Zeitung Online, 17.09.2015: www.faz.net/ aktuell/politik/denkich-an-deutschland-1/wenn-sys-temkritik-proletariat-und-mittelstand-eint-13797245.html [01.09.2019]

Fetscher, I., (1968). Von Marx zur Sowjetideologie, Frankfurt a. M. (Moritz Diesterweg). Fromm, E.: Gesamtausgabe in 12 Bänden [GA]. Edited by Rainer Funk, Stuttgart (DVA) 1999.

Fromm, E., (1922a). : Ein Prinzipielles Wort zur Erziehungsfrage, in: Jüdische Rundschau 103/104. Online: https://fromm-gesellschaft.eu/images/pdf-Dateien/1922a-deu.pdf [01.09.2019]

Fromm, E., 1930b: Der Staat als Erzieher. Zur Psychologie der Strafjustiz, GA 1, pp. 7–10; English:The State as Educator: On the Psychology of Criminal Justice, in: K. Anderson & R. Quinney (Eds.), Erich Fromm and Critical Criminology. Beyond the Punitive Society. Urbana (University of Illinois Press 2000), pp. 123–128.

Fromm, E., 1930d: :Ödipus in Innsbruck. Zum Halsmann-Prozess, GA 8, pp. 133–136.

Fromm, E., 1930e: Psychologie des Verbrechers und Strafvollzugsreform, in: Fromm

Forum [German Edition] Vol. 23, 2019, pp. 107–126.

Fromm, E., 1931a: Zur Psychologie des Verbrechers und der strafenden Gesellschaft, GA 1, pp. 11–30; English: On the Psychology of the Criminal and the Punitive Society, in: K. Anderson & R. Quinney (Eds.), Erich Fromm and Critical Crim-inology. Beyond the Punitive Society, Urbana (University of Illinois Press) 2000, pp. 129–156.

Fromm, E., 1931b: Politik und Psychoanalyse, GA 1, pp. 31–36; English: Politics and Psychoanalysis, in: S. E. Bronner & D. M. Kellner (Eds.), Critical Theory and Society. A Reader, New York (Routledge 1989), pp. 213–218.

Fromm, E., 1941a: Escape from Freedom, New York (Farrar and Rinehart) 1941. Fromm, E., 1963d: Disobedience as a Psychological and Moral Problem, in: C. Urquhart (Ed.), A Matter of Life, London (Jonathan Cape) 1963, pp. 97–105. Fromm, E., 1973a: The Anatomy of Human Destructiveness, New York (Holt, Rinehart and Winston) 1973.

Fromm, E., 1989b: Das Jüdische Gesetz. Zur Soziologie des Diaspora-Judentums, GA 12, pp. 19–126.

Fromm, E., 1992e: Die Determiniertheit der psychischen Struktur durch die Gesellschaft. Zur Methode und Aufgabe einer Analytischen Sozialpsychologie, GA 11, pp. 131–175); English: Man's impulse structure and its relation to culture [originated 1937], in: E. Fromm, Beyond Freud: From Individual to Social Psychoanalysis, New York (American Mental Health Foundation) 2010, pp. 17–74.

Fromm, E., & Maccoby, M., (1970b). Social Character in a Mexican Village. A Sociopsy-choanalytic Study, Englewood Cliffs (Prentice Hall) 1970.

Frommer, J., (2008). Vom eisernen zum gläsernen Gehäuse – Risiken persönlicher Identitätsentwicklung im Zeitalter der Globalisierung, in: M. Franz & J. Frommer, Medizin und Beziehung, Göttingen (Vandenhoeck und Ruprecht), pp. 29–55.

Frommer, J., Gallistl, A., Regner, F., & Lison, S. (2017). Nach den Haftunterlagen war das Verhalten der Klägerin problemlos ... Rückendeckung für die Diskreditierung von DDR-Unrechtsopfern durch richterliche Fehlbeurteilung in Sachsen-Anhalt: Ein Fallbericht, in: Trauma & Gewalt, Vol. 11 (No. 2), pp. 130–144.

Funk, R., (2011). Der entgrenzte Mensch. Warum ein Leben ohne Grenzen nicht frei, son- dern abhängig macht, Gütersloh (Gütersloher Verlagshaus).

Funk, R., (2019). Begrüßung und Einführung, in: Fromm Forum [German Edition], Vol. 23, pp. 9–12.

Gallistl, A., (2012). Die gesellschaftliche Bedingtheit der Psyche bei Erich Fromm. Diploma thesis in Economics, University of Trier.

Gallistl, A., (2014). Erich Fromms Studie Social Character in a Mexican Village. Einord- nung, Analyse und Diskussion von Fromms Versuch der Empirisierung seiner theore- tischen Konzeption und der Erprobung einer neuen empirischen Methodik. Master thesis Psychology, University of Trier. Online: http://www.fromm-gesellschaft.eu/ index.php/de/publikationen-blog/buecher/411-gallistl [01.09.2019]

Gallistl, A. (2020). Erich Fromm's Early Work on Criminal Justice. Its Historical and Current Significance. Fromm Forum (English Edition), 24, 80-100.

Hoffmann, A., & Leuschner, F. (2017). Rehabilitation und Entschädigung nach Vollstreck- ung einer Freiheitsstrafe und erfolgreicher Wiederaufnahme, Wiesbaden (Kriminolo- gische Zentralstelle).

Honneth, A., (2003). Umverteilung als Anerkennung. Eine Erwiderung auf Nancy Fraser, in; N. Fraser & A. Honneth, Umverteilung oder Anerkennung? Eine politisch-philosophische Kontroverse, Frankfurt a. M. (Suhrkamp), pp. 120–225.

Honneth, A. (Ed.), (2002). Befreiung aus der Mündigkeit. Paradoxien des gegenwärtigen Kapitalismus, Frankfurt a. M. (Campus).

Marcuse, H., (1958). Die Gesellschaftslehre des sowjetischen Marxismus (Soviet Marxism: A Critical Analysis), Neuwied (Hermann Luchterhand) 1964.

Marcuse, H., (1965). Repressive Toleranz (Repressive Tolerance), in: R. P. Wolff, B. Moore & H. Marcuse, Kritik der reinen Toleranz (Critique of Pure Tolerance), Frankfurt a.M. (Suhrkamp) 1968, pp. 91–128.

Marx, K. (1844) Ökonomisch-Philosophische Manuskripte, in: E. Fromm, Das Men- schenbild bei Marx (Marx's Concept of Man), Frankfurt a.M. (Ullstein) 1982, pp. 83–168.

Maté, G., & Maté, Daniel. (2022). The myth of normal : trauma, illness, and healing in a toxic culture / Gabor Maté, MD, with Daniel Maté. Avery, an imprint of Penguin Random House.

Schröter, M. (2015). Neue Details über die psychoanalytische Ausbildung von Erich Fromm (und Frieda Fromm-Reichmann), in: Fromm Forum [German Edition],Vol. 19, pp. 112–115.

Section 3
Real Life Stories

Maya Schenwar: https://truthout.org/section/prisons-and-policing/
https://www.youtube.com/watch?v=JFTRn_sIGiQ

Real Stories, B.E.S.:
https://www.cbc.ca/radio/asithappens/as-it-happens-friday-edition-1.4936736/man-raped-during-scared-straight-prison-tour-says-he-was-too-ashamed-to-tell-anyone-1.4936744

Real Stories, Billie McCune:
https://www.phaidon.com/agenda/photography/articles/2015/july/02/danny-lyons-conversa-tions-with-the-dead/

Real Stories, Jennifer Thomas:
https://www.youtube.com/watch?v=j8I749MuYbA

Real Stories, Jeff Wallace:
https://www.youtube.com/watch?v=TOxpjjzP6IM

Real Stories, Bianca Mercer:
https://thedeepmag.ca/aprisonpregnancy/
https://www.cbc.ca/radio/thecurrent/the-current-for-nov-29-2019-1.5378009/this-documentary-about-women-in-prison-handed-the-cameras-to-the-inmates-themselves-1.5378026

Real Stories, Julia Bilotta:

https://thedeepmag.ca/aprisonpregnancy/

https://scholars.wlu.ca/cgi/viewcontent.cgi?article=2980&context=etd

Real Stories, Unnamed Woman with Mental Health Impairment:

https://thedeepmag.ca/aprisonpregnancy/

Federally Sentenced Women in Canada:

https://www.oci-bec.gc.ca/cnt/priorities-priorites/women-femmes-eng.aspx

NWAC & Solitary Confinement:

https://www.nwac.ca/assets-knowledge-centre/NWAC-Indigenous-Women-in-Solitary-Confinement-Aug-22.pdf

Arbour, Louise. Commission of Inquiry into Certain Events at the Prison for Women in Kingston (Ottawa: Public Works and Government Services Canada, 1996) (Cat. No. JS42-73/1996E)

CAEFS and NWAC, "Women and the Canadian Legal System: Examining Situations of Hyper- Responsibility" Canadian Woman Studies (2008) 26.3-4

Canada - CSC, Coroner's Inquest Touching the Death of Ashley Smith - Jury Recommendations, (Ottawa: Public Safety Canada, 2013) retrieved online at http://www.csc- scc.gc.ca/publications/005007-9009-eng.shtml

Canada - CSC, Corrections and Conditional Release 2015 Annual Report: Statistical Overview (Ottawa: Public Safety Canada, 2016) retrieved online at https://www.publicsafety.gc.ca/cnt/rsrcs/pblctns/ccrso-2015/index-en.aspx

Canada - Corrections Canada, "Rates of Recidivism for Women Offenders" (2008) retrieved online at http://www.csc-scc.gc.ca/research/r192-eng.shtml

Canada - Minister of Justice, Corrections and Conditional Release Act (Ottawa: Justice Canada, 2017) retrieved online at http://laws-lois.justice.gc.ca/PDF/C-44.6.pdf

Canada - Office of the Prime Minister, "Minister of Justice and Attorney General Mandate Letter" (2015) retrieved online at http://pm.gc.ca/eng/minister-justice-and-attorney-general- canada-mandate-letter

Canada - Public Safety Canada, Corrections and Conditional Release: Statistical Overview (Ottawa: Public Safety Canada, 2015) retrieved online at https://www.publicsafety.gc.ca/cnt/rsrcs/pblctns/ccr-so-2015/ccrso-2015-en.pdf

Canada - Public Safety Canada, "Marginalized: The Aboriginal Women's experience in Federal Corrections" (2012) retrieved online at https://www.publicsafety.gc.ca/cnt/rsrcs/pblctns/mrgnlzd/index-en.aspx

Canada - Royal Commission on Aboriginal peoples, Report of the Royal Commission on Aboriginal Peoples - Volume 3: Gathering Strength (Ottawa: The Commission, 1996) retrieved online at http://data2.archives.ca/e/e448/e011188230-03.pdf

Canada - Statistics Canada, Study: Women in Canada: Women in the Criminal Justice System (Ottawa: Statistics Canada, 2017) Retrieved online at http://www.statcan.gc.ca/daily- quotidien/170606/dq170606a-eng.pdf

Canada - Sebastien April and Mylene Magrinelli Orsi for Department of Justice Canada, "Gladue Practices in the Provinces and Territories" (Ottawa: Research and Statistics Division, Department of Justice Canada, 2013) (Cat. No. J2-378/2013E-PDF)

Senate of Canada, Debates of the Senate - Standing Committee on Aboriginal Peoples (Vol. 150:63) retrieved online at http://publications.gc.ca/collections/collection_2016/sen/Y3-421-83- eng.pdf

Canadian Bar Association (15 April 2014), "Fifteen years after Gladue, What Progress?" [News Article]. Retrieved online at http://www.nationalmagazine.ca

Canadian Human Rights Commission, Report on the Equality Rights of Aboriginal People (2013) (Cat. No. HR4-22/2013E-PDF) Retrieved online at http://www.chrc- ccdp.gc.ca/sites/default/files/equality_aboriginal_report.pdf

CHRC, "Submission to the Committee Against Torture" (2012), retrieved online at http://www.chrc-ccdp.gc.ca/sites/default/files/cat_cct-eng.pdf

Harris, Kathleen, "Liberals set 15-day limit on solitary confinement of federal prisoners" CBC News (19 June 2017) Retrieved online at http://www.cbc.ca/news/politics/corrections-solitary- confine-ment-segregation-1.4167555

International Psychological Trauma Symposium, The Istanbul statement on the use and effects of solitary confinement (9 December 2007) Retrieved online at http://solitaryconfinement.org/

NWAC, Federally-Sentenced Women Offenders: An Issue Paper (2007), retrieved online at www.nwac.ca

NWAC, Aboriginal Women and the Legal Justice System in Canada: An Issue Paper (2007), retrieved online at www.nwac.ca

NWAC and Justice For Girls, Gender Matters: Building Strength in Reconciliation, (2012), retrieved online at https://www.nwac.ca/policy-areas/human-rights-in-canada/justice/

NWAC and Justice For Girls, Gender Matters: Summary dialogue report of the cross country Arrest the Legacy: from Residential Schools to Prisons dialogues (2015), retrieved online at https://www.nwac.ca/wp-content/uploads/2015/05/Gender-Matters-Introduction.pdf

McIvor, Sharon and Johnson, Ellisa C. (for NWAC). Detailed Position of the Native Women's Association of Canada on the Complaint Regarding the Discriminatory Treatment of Federally Sentenced Women by the Government of Canada filed by the Canadian Association of Elizabeth Fry Societies. (5 May 2003) Retrieved from https://www.nwac.ca/wp- content/uploads/2015/05/2003-NWAC-Position-on-the-Treatment-of-Federally-Sentenced- Women.pdf

Méndez, Juan. Torture and other cruel, inhuman or degrading treatment or punishment: Note by the Secretary-General (United Nations General Assembly, sixty-sixth session, 2011). Retrieved from http://undocs.org/A/66/268

Monture, Patricia A., "Women and Risk: Aboriginal Women, Colonialism and Correctional Practice" in First Voices: An Aboriginal Women's Reader by Patricia A. Monture and Patricia D. McGuire (Eds.) (Toronto: Inanna Publications and Education Inc., 2009) originally published in 1999 in Canadian Woman Studies.

Monture, Patricia A. Thunder in My Soul: A Mohawk Woman Speaks (Halifax: Fernwood Publishing, 2002)

Monchalin, Lisa, The Colonial Perspective: An Indigenous Perspective on Crime and Injustice in Canada (Toronto: University of Toronto Press, 2016)

Office of the Correctional Investigator, Spirit Matters: Aboriginal People and the Corrections and Conditional Release Act (Ottawa: Minister of Public Works and Government Services Canada, 2012) (CAT. NO.: PS104-6/2013E-PDF)

Office of the Correctional Investigator [Press Release], "Office of the Correctional Investigator Releases Administrative Segregation in Federal Corrections: 10 Year Trends Federal Corrections Overuses Segregation to Manage Inmates" (Ottawa: The Correctional Investigator Canada, 28 May 2015)

Ontario Human Rights Commission, Supplementary Submission of the Ontario Human Rights Commission to the Ministry of Community Safety and Correctional Services' Provincial Segregation Review (2016) retrieved online at www.ohrc.on.ca

Parkes, Debra "Cruel and unusual punishment: It's time to end solitary confinement" The Globe and Mail (6 June 2016) retrieved online at www.theglobeandmail.com

Pate, Kim [Speech] "Increasing over-representation of Indigenous women in Canadian Prisons" (Debate of the Senate, 1st Session, 42nd Parliament, December 2016).

R v. Gladue, [1999] 1 S.C.R. 688

Sapers, Howard, Annual Report of the Office of the Correctional Investigator 2015-2016 (Ottawa: The Correctional Investigator Canada, 2016) Cat. No.: PS100E-PDF, retrieved online.

Shalev, Sharon. A Sourcebook on Solitary Confinement (London: London School of Economics and Political Science, 2008). Retrieved online at http://solitaryconfinement.org

United Nations, The United Nations Standard Minimum Rules for the Treatment of Prisoners (the Nelson Mandela Rules) (2015). Retrieved from https://www.unodc.org/documents/justice- and-prison-reform/GA-RESOLUTION/E_ebook.pdf

United Nations General Assembly, United Nations Rules for the Protection of Juveniles Deprived of their Liberty (A/RES/45/113) (1990). Retrieved online at http://www.un.org/documents/ga/res/45/a45r113.htm

United Nations Human Rights Committee, (10 March 1992) "CCPR General Comment No. 20: Article 7 (Prohibition of Torture, or Other Cruel, Inhuman or Degrading Treatment or Punishment)", 44th Session of the Human Rights Committee.. Retrieved online at http://www.refworld.org/docid/453883fb0.html

United Nations, "The United Nations Standard Minimum Rules for the Treatment of Prisoners (the Nelson Mandela Rules)" (2015), retrieved online at https://www.unodc.org/

United Nations General Assembly, "United Nations Rules for the Treatment of Women Prisoners and Non-custodial Measures for Women Offenders (the Bangkok Rules)" A/RES/65/229 (2011). Retrieved online at https://www.unodc.org/documents/justice-and-prison- reform/Bangkok_Rules_ENG_22032015.pdf

United Nations International Covenant on Civil and Political Rights, "Concluding observations on the sixth periodic report of Canada" (2015) retrieved online at http://tbinternet.ohchr.org/_layouts/treatybodyexternal/Download.aspx?symbolno=CCPR%2FC %2FCAN%2FCO%2F6&Lang=en

Section 4
Possibilities

Boen, C. E., Olson, H., & Lee, H. (2022). Vicarious exposure to the criminal legal system among parents and siblings. Journal of Marriage and Family, 84(5), 1446–1468. https://doi.org/10.1111/jomf.12842

Caldwell, B. (2021). The Twice Diminished Culpability of Juvenile Accomplices to Felony Murder. UC Irvine Law Review, 11(4), 905.

Campaign For Youth Justice: https://www.campaignforyouthjustice.org/news/blog/item/stories-from-mothers-of-incarcerated-youth

Crowell, N. A., Widom, C. S., & McCord, J. (2001). Juvenile Crime, Juvenile Justice. National Academies Press. https://doi.org/10.17226/9747

Lee, H., & Wildeman, C. (2021). Assessing mass incarceration's effects on families. Science (American Association for the Advancement of Science), 374(6565), 277–281. https://doi.org/10.1126/science.abj7777

Letter re Youth Incarceration: https://www.law.georgetown.edu/icap/wp-content/uploads/sites/32/2022/02/Letter-re-Juvenile-Life-Without-Parole-in-the-Federal-System-2.17.22.pdf

Locking Up Children in the USA | Visiting Juvenile Prison: American Incarceration System Documentary: Java Films (Java Discover) https://www.youtube.com/watch?v=LGg8RLjLCSQ

Mate, G., (2012), Talk at Bioneers: https://www.youtube.com/watch?v=erZhTPkOLb0

Maté, G., & Maté, D. (2022). The myth of normal : trauma, illness, and healing in a toxic culture / Gabor Maté, MD, with Daniel Maté. Avery, an imprint of Penguin Random House.

Pickett, K., & Wilkinson, R. (2010). The Spirit Level. Penguin Books. https://equalitytrust.org.uk

Prison Testimonies of Torture: https://www.afsc.org/sites/default/files/documents/Survivors%20 Speak%20-%20AFSC%20CAT%20Shadow%20Report%202014.pdf

Sirois, C. (2020). The strain of sons' incarceration on mothers' health. Social Science & Medicine (1982), 264, 113264–113264. https://doi.org/w10.1016/j.socscimed.2020.113264

Townsend, Jonathan (2022). On Community: https://www.youtube.com/watch?v=QJHQmC-JMtZY&list=RDCMUCxr2d4As312LulcajAkKJYw&index=12

"Turnaround's end". Huntsville Forester. Metroland Media Group. December 5, 2003. UN: https://www.afsc.org/document/survivors-speak-prisoner-testimonies-torture-united-states-prisons-and-jails

Turney, K., & Jackson, D. B. (2021). Mothers' health following youth police stops. Preventive Medicine, 150, 106693–106693. https://doi.org/10.1016/j.ypmed.2021.106693

United Nations Convention on the Rights of the Child. For more information, see https://www.ohchr.org/en/instruments-mechanisms/instruments/convention-rights-child.

UN Press Release on Solitary Confinement: For more information, see: https://www.ohchr.org/en/press-releases/2020/02/united-states-prolonged-solitary-confinement-amounts-psychological-torture

Wildeman, C., & Lee, H. (2021). Women's Health in the Era of Mass Incarceration. Annual Review of Sociology, 47(1), 543–565. https://doi.org/10.1146/annurev-soc-081320-113303

Zehr, H. (2016). The little book of restorative justice. Good Books.

♦

"Only as we live by imagination can we truly be said to live at all."

~ *Neville Goddard (1905-1972)*
Humanist Philosopher & Mystic

Poppy Publishing, Ltd.
www.poppypublishing.ca

"The function of the artist in a disturbed society is to ask the right questions, to open consciousness, and elevate the mind."

~ *Marina Abramović*
Conceptual and Performace Artist

www.ingramcontent.com/pod-product-compliance
Lightning Source LLC
Chambersburg PA
CBHW040844120626
46547CB00001B/25